Nobody's Daughter

Angel Novak

Order this book online at www.trafford.com
or email orders@trafford.com

Most Trafford titles are also available at major online book retailers.

Printed in the United States of America.

ISBN: 978-1-4907-3617-4 (sc)
ISBN: 978-1-4907-3616-7 (e)

Trafford rev. 05-12-2014

www.trafford.com
North America & international
toll-free: 1 888 232 4444 (USA & Canada)
fax: 812 355 4082

First and foremost I would like to thank my father God for being with me throughout the traumatic events that were my life. And giving me the many blessings and experiences I did have. Second I would like to thank my sons, Bug and Tommy-without whom I would never have had a reason, or been forced to produce the strength I needed to make it through. I love you both with every beat of my heart. I will always believe in you and stand behind you in whatever you do in life. Isaiah and Joshua- your gramma loves you so much, you make grammas heart smile. I owe a huge thank you to all four of my sisters. They have been there for me in every way possible through all of the craziness and chaos bad decisions in my entire life and loved me no matter what. We have fought, cried, laughed, loved and lost together. You have all been a wonderful influence on my life and I am so thankful and blessed to have you all for my sisters. And finally I would like to thank the rest of my family and the many awesome friends who have been here for me and loved me even when I was unlovable.

Nobody's Daughter

I was born on August 3rd, 1968 in the back of a red '59 Chevy on Highway 55 in Chicago Illinois. I should have known by the way things had started out it was going to be a rough ride, but I decided to stick it out anyway. My mom was a twenty year old drug addicted, Paranoid Schizophrenic, and my dad was a 21 year old drug addicted burglar, and convicted murderer. Wasn't that an interesting combination for a couple of young kids having some kids? My prospects were looking a little dim, I didn't know that yet though. Mom was young, going through a lot of problems with her own family life when she met my dad. She had lost her father when she was only 11 years old. He was an architect and a mathematician, in St. Louis. She was his only child and he had spoiled her rotten. Their story reminded me of that Shirley Temple movie, "Poor Little Rich Girl". After treating my mother like a princess for her first 11 years, he died suddenly, and left her with my grandmother, who had the personality and heartfelt warmth of a potato, so mom didn't have a whole lot to start with as far as how to be a loving mother.

Not only did mom already have a 2 year old baby at home when I was born, (my older sister, Heather), but she had other deep seeded issues. She had also given birth to a little boy when she was 15 years old, and was forced to give him up for adoption. She just had so much stuff going on for her age when I showed up, I am sure she was less than thrilled to say the least. Her own mother had put her out of their house after she had her first child. The baby's father was also young and he just said, "the baby wasn't his." Back then they did not have DNA tests to prove who his father was so the responsibility of the whole situation fell onto my 15 year old mother.

Mom had no parents, or family support to help her. She was just young, alone and lost. She was forced to live with relatives during her pregnancy of my brother, and was treated like a Piranha by the family she did have. After my brothers birth my grandmother told her she was moving and my mom couldn't go. She was only 15 years old, when she tried to go back to school, but she was told that she was too old and could not attend. In the early 60's giving birth out of wedlock, was considered the ultimate sin and one was to be ashamed and shun. This is pretty much the only background information I have on her, or any explanation I have for her behavior. She never really told me much as we were never very close or shared anything intimate. I guess that's how she ended up with my dad, because she didn't have anywhere else to go, was very young, and didn't what else to do.

I think she met my dad at a gas station, and they just ended up together. The last thing she really didn't needed was another child. I seriously doubt I was planned because my dad told me once that there was a really good chance that I was conceived in the same car I was born in. I actually thought that was pretty funny and hey, it was the 60's. Apparently dad wasn't all that excited about my upcoming arrival either. He didn't even get up to take her to the hospital when she went into labor with me until her water broke. Mom had told me all of my life that she was in labor for 30 minutes and it was a 45 minute trip to the hospital. My dad told me when I was 26 that he was just an asshole, and wouldn't get up and take her to the hospital. Hence the mobile delivery room.

So dads driving, no doubt moms yelling, and when I was born I just landed on the back floorboard and they left me there until we got to the hospital. No one cleared my airway or smacked me and made me cry (that comes later in the story, be patient), so I didn't breathe right away. This is why I believe I have had lung problems throughout my entire life. I had pneumonia 7 times before the age of five. I was told I spent a lot of time in the hospital as a baby, I can't remember that far back, but judging by my lungs now I believe them. I was a small, sickly, quiet child. I didn't say much, just quietly observed all of the crazy stuff going on around me. I guess when you just ignore kids for so long when they're small they learn not to ask one for anything. I learned early on to just go find what I needed in life, because complaining or whining wouldn't have helped.

Dad stayed around for a couple of years, he was in, and out of prison as well as our lives. I don't recall him being around except for a couple small memories' don't really have bad memories, I just don't recall him being there. I don't know what it feels like to have parents that are happy to see you, read stories, have bath time, family dinners, hugs, or feel love. I am sure other people grow up with a warm family life where everyone spends time together and laughs. That was not in my childhood though, we existed, basically on auto-pilot, mostly alone, and unloved. I do not remember any love in my house at all when I was growing up. Just stress, anger, and loneliness

Apparently my dad was very physically abusive to my mom. My sister Heather, said she remembered them fighting, and stuff, but either I was too little or just blocked it out, I do have large holes in my memories as a child so anything is possible. I don't think he was mean to us kids on purpose. He was just lost in a whirlwind of drugs, alcohol, violence, and chasing other women. I guess parenting 2 daughters and caring for a young wife didn't fit into that lifestyle. I do remember my mom sleeping a LOT and being alone a lot, just kind of wandering around the house with very little light, not much to do, and no one to talk too. We learn to find food, watch TV, and simply exist. It seems sad and depressing, and it may have been, but I had never seen anything else so it didn't bother me as much as it should have. The parents just kind of did their own thing and we found a way to survive. Someday we had a dad, and some days we didn't. Mom was there, but she wasn't. It was what it was.

So then, somehow Mom decided when I was 3 that she didn't care for men anymore. I don't know how in the world that came about but dad was in prison again, and then all of a sudden one day she brought this new girlfriend home. It was kind of like you have a new daddy now, but different. Her name was Dusty, we lived in a very small apartment. They use to take us to the zoo, and church, and somewhat normal family outings. I guess they thought we were too young to figure out much, but like I said, it was a very small apartment. I suppose she was an alright person I don't recall her being mean to us, she didn't stay around long. It was probably just until dad got out of prison for a while.

I don't remember that actual homecoming, but I bet it was interesting. Dad showed back up one day, he just did that from time to time, and came back home for another short period of time.

Mom and dad were on drugs, but now mom had a new hobby . . . . She had decided to become a devil worshipper. She pulled back the living room carpet, painted a big white star on our floor, lit a whole bunch of candles all around the star, and would sit completely naked in the middle of it chanting or something weird. Dad was also in his own world he was breaking into houses, pharmacies, being shot by the police, getting arrested, and beating the crap out of my mom. It is hard to describe, or explain their behavior, and activities at this time. It was just a tornado of weird shit. My sister Heather and I just sat on the couch and watched. It didn't seem like they were even aware we were there. I guess I was around 4 when he left again. We never knew why he kept leaving or where he was going, so I don't think I felt anything about it. Neither one of them really talked to us, it's not like we had any type of normal family habits anyway.

We did go to see him down at the city jail, it was back when they had open windows with bars on them so it must have been summer time. He had a long string tied onto a candy bar wrapper. He lowered it down to where mom, and us kids were standing on the ground under his window in his cell. Mom said, she was putting quarters in the wrapper so he could use a vending machine or something. Now I think she was putting drugs or money in it. We were too young to know any better. Jails were ran a lot different in the 60's and 70's He was gone for good after that. Then one day mom ran out of drugs and took us over to their drug dealers house to get some more. I don't remember this being the reason we were going there, but that's what my older sister told me. She pulled up with us in the backseat, and said, "George said you might be able to help me out". He told her "come here sugar, I got what you need".

Next thing we knew they were married and mom told us we had a new dad, (it was a guy this time), his name was Cletus. My grandma-(my mom's mother) use to keep Heather all the time, who was 21 months older than I. I guess she couldn't find a babysitter for me, so I got to go with them on their honeymoon. They went to some small motel that had a little room with a loveseat on the corner, where I slept. ALL they did is sleep. They never got out of bed or took care of me anyway. I don't know how long we were there, but I was 4 yrs. old, bored, and starving. Since I was used to doing for myself, one morning while they were sleeping

I took some money they had left lying around. It was probably just a couple dollars, but I went looking around the place. I snuck out of the room, wandered up, and down some halls until I finally found a kitchen and some old lady made me toast. I got to eat, and was happy for a minute until they finally figured out which room I was in, and returned me. The hotel employee had to knock on our door for a while trying to get my mom and Cletus to wake up and open it. They kept yelling out for them to, "Wait a minute", until the people finally explained that they had their kid out there in the hallway. Actually, I think that part was kind of funny now that I look back on it. I guess I have a sort of a warped little sense of humor. Mom and Cletus were so mad that I had left the room even though they did not notice I was gone until someone brought me back, I got whooped for leaving the room, and for stealing money. Ok, that part wasn't quite as funny. Like it was my fault they left me unfed and unattended.

Apparently my new "dad" didn't have a place to live because he moved in with mom, Heather and I at my real dad's parent's house. Grandma and grandpa owned a house they didn't live in at the time, and was letting my mom stay there with us kids because she didn't have a place either. Obviously mom didn't ask permission to bring her new husband home to stay. I can't imagine what she was thinking, and she knew my grandparents were crazy. She knew my dad was crazy. Maybe she thought my dad would be locked up forever, or maybe she was just stupid or crazy herself. I will never know, but that was kind of ballsy to move her new man into his parents' house. I found out later Cletus sold drugs from the house. I never noticed this when we were living there, but when I was older I went by that house with a friend of mine. He said, "hey I use to buy dope off a guy named Cletus Joe in that house back in the day." My grandma also told me when I was older the same thing. Mom would never admit to something like that. Life was perfect back then, if you ask her.

I don't even recall being inside that house much, so either I didn't spend a lot of time in there, or it was just so bad somehow I chose not to remember any of it. Either way it works for me. Most of the time they would just lock us out of the house since it was summer, we didn't care much. There were a bunch of other kids to play with around there. All our neighbors around us had vegetable gardens in their backyards, and apple trees and stuff. My sister Heather was 6, and she would take me around throughout the day and get me vegetables to eat, drinks from the house, and play. Poor little thing, the whole responsibility of my care and safety had fallen on her young, inept shoulders.

One day her friend invited her over to spend the night. Since we were locked out of the house anyway, she just took me with her, and we stayed the night. In the morning we came back home and were all scared we were going to get in so much trouble. Fortunately, hadn't even noticed we were gone. I was 4 years old, when my grandma finally came to the realization, that my mom had moved her new husband into their home, and literally threw them out of her house. Mom and grandma had a huge confrontation in the front yard. I remember grandma yelling at my mom about all the things she was doing, and while I didn't really understand what was going on, I knew we had to go. I guess mom and Cletus did not want to leave, and I still cannot imagine why they thought they should be allowed to stay. My Grandma was really mad, and told my mom she was lucky my dad was in prison or he would kill the both of them. My Grandmother said Heather and I could stay, but mom and her drug dealing husband was to leave immediately.

Of course, Mom took us with her moving around all over the place. We traveled like gypsies, never knowing where we would end up, or how long we would stay. We were too young to realize this was not normal. Mom would come back to our grandma every now and then, and drop us off for Grandma to babysit. Sometimes she would leave us for as long as 2 months. Bless her heart, my Grandma Eaton means the world to me, and I appreciate, so much of all she did for us. My mother made her life harder than it already was. I know that lady loved me, and I love her so much.(I love you grandma.) Mom and Cletus were running around doing their thing not worried about us. Until finally mom would decide it was time to get us back. She would be embarrassed to come and claim us after being gone so long. So, she would call the police and have they come go over and pick us up. A couple of times she would leave us at people's houses so long, they would just drop us off at the police station, and have somebody come to get us. I do remember that happening, but I was too young to know what they were doing with us. Child abuse and neglect laws were not enforced very well back in the 70's. Even though my sister, and I never saw our mother and Cletus doing drugs would later in life find out they were doing a Amphetamine, called Preluden. They lived a very strange life, so we all lived a very strange life.

It seemed like they drove around a lot, when they shouldn't have, because there were a lot of car accidents. There were many times I recall, sitting in the back of an ambulance waiting for my Uncle Mike to come and pick me up. He would show up to rescue me at the very time I needed it, and he made me feel safe. I would be sitting there, young, scared, little, and alone, and, all of a sudden I would see my Uncle Mike come up to the ambulance and get me. I knew things were going to be ok, and I was safe then, at least up to that point. I didn't know what was going to happen, or even what was happening right then for that matter.

There was one time in particular that I was really scared. Mom and Cletus were acting so weird after the accident. Being a child I don't know if the paramedics, police or who, but someone, had my mom strapped down to a stretcher, it didn't seem like she wanted to be there. One of her legs was pinned behind her somehow, and she kept yelling, "kill em Cletus" I didn't see or hear anything going on that would cause her to say something like that. I realize now that it must have been the drugs, I don't think she even knew I was standing there watching her. I was too young to have a clue what was going on and that did terrify me.

5

Times, I know were different back then, but I think things were more different for our family than it was for others. Heather and I didn't have friends coming over, and staying the night. We did play with neighbor kids during the day, and I remember, once Heather had her best friend Laurie come over. The little friend ask us, "How comes you guys don't ever have dinner?" We didn't even know people sat down around 5:00 pm and ate dinner together. Heather didn't even know what the girl meant. She didn't usually have a friends over to the house, but I guess Laurie was around her so much she didn't think anything of it.

Our parents were gone most of the time, and they never had babysitters for us, so we were left home alone all by ourselves; and that was terrifying. Being so young and small we quietly listen for every sound, because we were scared someone was going to break into the house, and do God knows what to us. After spending the entire evening looking out the window watching for them to come home we would sleep together huddled closely in one bed clutching all the weapons, and things to protect us that two little girls could think of.

There was an all-night laundromat, a block, or so from our house. Nobody, thought anything about sending my sister, and I down to do laundry alone. It did not matter what time of night it was, and since the basket was so heavy we had to drag it to the laundromat. Our parents never realized if it was night or day, because they were high all the time, and didn't really know or care what time it was. We were just two little girls, but we learned how to be survivors at an early age.

I was very underweight, and sick all the time. A lot of it was my lungs, but I had stomach problems too. I'm sure now that it was from the stress of having them argue and being hungry all the time. It was sad and stressful, and most likely a lot harder for my sister. She was living the same hard life I way I was, but she also had the responsibility of taking care of me, and all my needs too. She was all I had, but she was enough.

After they would, finally fall asleep, we would wash a dish to eat out of, and then steal their change, and go to the corner store alone to get food. I cannot remember where we lived at, since we had moved around so much. I do remember we ended up in an upstairs apartment, with long wooden steps going down the back into a large back yard. The yard was full of junk. Cletus turned out to be very abusive too, he drank all the time, yelled at mom, and hit her. He became more and more irritable to her. It was a rat hole city apartment, with a rat for my mom's husband.

I was 4 years old the day they were standing in the apartment arguing, and Cletus just pulled out a gun, and out of nowhere, shot my mom in the leg. I know one would think there would be so much more to say about that incident in itself, but maybe I have become numb about some of the horrible things that happened when I was little. It just doesn't seem real. It isn't because I don't care about my mother, because I love her very much, and hate what she had to go through, because of the things she did. I am unable still, to process this incident though.

Heather and I were just sitting there watching of course. That whole moment in time was so weird, I'm not sure if it was shock, or some involuntary self-defense mechanism . . . . I can remember the entire situation as far as what I could see, but not any sound. They told us to each grab a toy to bring, and get in their van, we all moved around, and went in some sort of robotic fashion not in a panic, because my mother had just been shot in front of us the way you would expect people to do. Cletus casually announced "we got to run to the hospital". I brought a matchbox car and my sister brought a little Gumby like action figure, and we played with them on the back floorboard of the van until we got there and patched mom up. And then we went on with our lives like it never happened.

Of course, no one ever explained what was going on in our house we just existed from day to day with no event, or meaning. Nothing specific to mark any moment in time, we just were. I was lonely and scared and sad. I didn't even know at the time that Cletus was not only molesting my sister, but he would bring his brother Freddie over so he could abuse her as well. She told me later that he would have her do things, and tell her, "if you don't do it I will just have to make Angel do it", So she would protect me, and it not only hurts that my sister had to go through something like that, but I feel horrible guilt that she had to do it, because of me. I know that the fault only lies with my stepdad, but he did use her love for me to get her to comply. When she did go to my mom and try to tell her about it, my mom just told her not to make her life any harder than it already was. So my sister Heather, did not bring it up again, and lived with that horrible part of her life in silence.

Cletus rarely came home from work, and when he did he was mean drunk. He refused to give my mom money for the bills. I was the only one in the house he wasn't mean as hell too. I was a little scrawny, kind of cute kid, and he liked me. Lucky, for me not in a sexual way. He would come by give me a wad of money, or bring me a new TV, or a bike, and treat everyone else like shit. Then he would leave.

My mom got to hating me pretty early.

Whenever mom was high I guess she would do very strange things. Heather, and I had a small record player, and we had the theme song from the Lone Ranger show (William Tell Overture). She would make us sit there and play the record over and over again all night, because it made her paint faster. We thought that was a little strange, but we laughed at her when she was doing that all the time. She looked so damn stupid. She would paint the outside of our house, the inside of our house . . . whatever, she tweaked on painting. But she never finished any area that she started painting. So just to give you some kind of idea—the outside of our house was like red on the bottom corner, blues up at the top, and white in the middle. Not in any kind of pattern, just a bunch of paint all over the building. It is really unbelievable that she did stuff like that. As uppity as she is now, and so far in denial about the things she did in the past, those memories are funny as shit. She may have taken every ounce of pride, self-respect, dignity, and happiness I had at the time, but she can never take the memories I have of her acting like a complete idiot all those years.

If that wasn't embarrassing enough, when, on the rare occasion we did bring a friend over, mom would climb behind some furniture and try to hold conversations with people in the room, like crouched down behind the couch or something. Try and explain that to your friends when you don't even understand it yourself. We would try to play it off like mom just had a sense of humor, or thought she was funny, but, hey, when your mom's behind the couch talking people kind of know something's up. Some days I would go to school in the morning, and live at one house, and then when we got out of school we had moved, and we lived somewhere else. We would walk in, and everything in the house was in a big pile in the living room floor telling us, we live here now. In my mind I was thinking, oh, cool-another school this month. When I was 7 we moved to Compton Street, a four family flat. The next door neighbors were very nice to us. They would come out and talk to my sister, and I when we were out in the yard. We lived in the upstairs apartment, with a bunch of stairs that went down to our lower porch. We were talking to the neighbors one afternoon, when all of a sudden, my mom yells, "somebody help me", and then she came flying down the stairs. One minute we were all standing on the porch talking, and the next here she came while we all just looked open mouthed, not knowing what was happening, or what to do. Cletus had beaten her up again, and broke her arm. He just stood there, and acted like nothing had ever happened.

They use to have horrible fights all the time, and mom would tell him she wanted him to move out. Then he would say that he didn't want to leave us kids. She'd say that we wanted him to go too. Then came that big argument where they would call us downstairs even if they had to drag us out of bed, and ask us if we wanted him to stay or go. There is no right answer to this question, because he inevitably was going to stay. If we said we wanted him to go, then he was mad, and if we said we wanted him to stay then mom was mad. Either way we ended up looking like the assholes at the end of the argument. If we could have been honest we would have told them, we wished they would both go.

Cletus also use to play softball, and he would always pick me up, and take me to his games. After the games he would take me to hang out at the bars all day. When I would get home, he would drop me off, and mom would beat me with whatever she could find because, I let him go to the bar and drink. When I was approximately nine years old when she beat the shit out of me, in front of our neighbors with a wooden tennis racket, because I went to the bar with him. It wasn't like I was driving or had a choice. I just tried to run away from her crying, but since I wasn't allowed to leave the yard, I really got beaten all around it. I knew she was really mad at me, but I didn't know what it was that I was supposed to do. I use to be so embarrassed to even look at the neighbors, and I knew they had to see what she was doing to me. They never said anything to anyone to help. They didn't really talk to us, at all by this point.

Cletus had a very large family. Mom didn't really go around her family for holidays or anything. I don't think they liked her. And he had no other children, and even though they had us call him dad, we were step kids over there. They treated us just like you would expect people like that to treat step kids. Every Christmas they would dress us up all in fancy dresses, curl our hair and make us look nice. However, when we got there the tree would be all decorated with presents all around it. A huge feast and holiday party filled with everyone dressed in their Christmas best. Only the presents were for the real kids, we were only step kids so we didn't get them.

I don't even know why they would take us over there every year and put us though that it was so hurtful and made us feel like nothing. We were young and would always ask, "where's our presents?", because we didn't know any better. They never got us any presents and for 10 years we had to enjoy this Christmas tradition. One year mom "forgot" Christmas. She had decorated a tree, got everyone's hopes up, and then didn't remember to buy presents for us or have a holiday meal, or any type of celebration. I guess she was high that year. My sister and I woke up that morning, and looked at our tree with nothing under it. We waited, and waited . . . then just sat there feeling horrible all day knowing it was Christmas; just not for us. That was pretty pitiful, and she felt bad enough after that, and she took out a small credit union loan every year and got us something. It is a wonder I even like Christmas at all anymore. We were unable to forget the forgotten Christmas though. We asked her about it later, and she said she had money, she didn't know why she had done that. I am hoping at least some drugs were involved in that incident and she wasn't just being an asshole.

Soon it was time for us to move again. The house on Iowa street was a very scary, strange house. It was just so dark and creepy, the basement looked like it was haunted. I lived there for 4 years, the longest I had ever lived anywhere. It had 3 floors, with mom and Cletus's bedroom upstairs. Next to their room was the room Heather and I shared. The downstairs had a kitchen and living room, I guess it seemed bigger back then, because it did not seem like it was such a small house, but in reality it was. The basement had a great big old wooden door leading to the outside that did not lock or even close properly most of the time. I spent an immense time down there doing laundry at night, and was so scared. Our bathroom was down there too. I think it was because the house was so old it was built with no bathroom and it had been added on later. So you had to walk all the way down to that creepy basement to go to the bathroom in the middle of the night. Oh I hated that house. I can not remember one good day there.

Mom was still a tweaker, in other words, an addict. Cletus hung out 24/7 at a bars up the street. Mom would make her rounds at night trying to find him so she would drive around to all the bars and have us kids go in, and try to flush him out. Sometimes my sister and I would go sit up there and do shots with him when we skipped school in our catholic school uniforms. I was only 12 or 13 years old, but no one ever cared that we were kids drinking in a bar. One could not do something like that now. Mom use to send me all over the neighborhood day or night to get whatever she wanted, or needed. I got my first curfew ticket at 11 p.m. buying my mom a pack of cigarettes I was so scared to even be out there at night.

I guess tweaker heads think it's funny to freak out little kids, for example. Mom would send me to the basement in the middle of the night and I had to go outside to get to it when I would come back up the basement stairs, she would jump out, and scare the crap out of me. When we had to go to bed at night, Cletus would hide in our closet, and jump out and act like he was a vampire. I had nightmares all the time when I was little, and still do sometimes. For obvious reasons, vampires freak me out.

I am sure, because of the drugs, my parents were somewhat delusional, and acted very strange. Mom would get all geeked out and be convinced we had done something we didn't really do. One day she came home and accused us of being on the roof while she was gone. We said," of course, we had not been on the roof." So she took turns beating us with a belt all day until "we told the truth." After a couple hours we were thinking, well, maybe if we confessed we were on the roof she would quit smacking us. She would hit me with the belt for a while, and then switch to my sister for a while. It's a wonder she didn't get worn out from all that work. We were screaming, and crying the whole time, and terrified because we didn't know what was going on. We didn't know what was wrong with her at this point. Finally, we just told her fine we was on the roof and we didn't get hit anymore.

When I turned 12 years old, my mom found religion. She made this big production of confessing to us that she had been using drugs. We were so happy to find out she wasn't just batshit crazy, but there was some type of explanation for all her weird ass shit. We actually felt a lot better, but now she was just batshit crazy, and religious. We liked her better high as strange as that may sound. She had not spent any time, or effort training us on how to behave, and then got mad at because we didn't automatically act like all the other perfect little kids from her new church. How were we supposed to have any idea how to be? We had never even had real parents it was painfully obvious that we disgusted her in comparison, and she was downright ashamed of us. The only part of the Bible she felt the need to abide by was "spare the rod, and spoil the child", she had no clue what she was doing.

My sister would never stand still to be whooped. I was little and scared. Mom would use one of those long metal spatulas that was made for cooking to beat me. She would hit me all over so bad it would cut my clothes, and my arms as I would try to block the blows. I was going to St. Thomas School at the time.

I did not have many really close friends that knew anything about my home life, or me. I had a few friends who would invite me over to lunch and I would go and eat with them amazed at the quiet houses that had food in them. I went to school every day with cuts and bruises all over me. No one ever said a word. A couple of people knew what was happening because it was so obvious, but nobody knew what to do. I did not tell people but they could see the marks. It was very embarrassing and I did not know how to explain to people that I had cuts and bruises all over my arms because my mother hated me. I was too ashamed. I never considered the fact that the shame should have been hers. In my 8th grade school picture I have her handprint on my face.

Mom made Cletus move out of the house, after she found religion, or he just left, I don't know. He was rarely home anyway, no one even noticed the difference. Mom was going to church all the time and bringing all kinds of weird people home with her. Like many of the other odd things that woman did, I didn't get this new thing either. She brought this one guy she had found somewhere sniffing glue, and had him stay with the three of us so he could get saved or something. Then she brought some alcoholic Catholic priest home. After that, she brought one of my dad's friends home to stay for a while, he ended up beating the living shit out of her so he left. There were all kinds of guys she brought home to stay talking about, she was converting somebody. I guess she was happier and had found some type of peace for herself. She still was a Paranoid Schizophrenic who refused to get help for it, and had behavior we could ever understand. However, she never, gave any thought to what she was supposed to do with her two teenaged daughters who very badly needed a mother, and the need to feel any type of love at all. We were starved for love and acceptance. We had to go to her church and pretend we were as happy as everyone else when inside we were lost, and just sad. She just never had any love for us. We felt as if we were just a burden she had been stuck with. Heather and I always said we wished she would just go drop us off somewhere and leave us. She did not like us she did not want to be responsible for us, and we obviously was not good enough for her. She let us know that on a regular basis. I have never had the sort of bond with her that a mother and child has. It just never happened.

Soon after Cletus left, our gas got turned off later learned he died of a liver disease cause by alcoholism. I guess we could not afford to get the gas turned back on. Mom put one of those big metal tubs in the hallway and heated up water to bathe, and we had a space heater, and blankets over doorways. I imagine mom was feeling very frustrated and overwhelmed by this point. Right about then, my dad's brother Uncle Billy, and my grandpa get snot, slinging drunk, and decide to come to our house around three o'clock in the morning because they want to visit us girls. Mom did not want them in her house, but they had a gun so she had to let them come talk to us. We did not know what to think, as we were half asleep in our pajamas sitting on the edge of our beds talking. As they came in they explained, "We love you guys, and just wanted to see you." After they left, my sister, and I got beaten, because they had come by to see us. Hey thanks for that memory.

Dad was in prison for murder. We went to a catholic school, and had to lie about why we did not have a dad. There was a large amount of shame to having a father who was in prison, and for murder no less. Even though we did have a stepdad, we were not supposed to tell anyone, because we were on a school scholarship. The school had punishers too, and a lot of our punishment was having to kneel for long periods of time on the ground. Just kneeling there for as long as they said we had too, no matter how long. My mom use to make me do it outside. I really, really, hated that part. This lady would have me out in the middle of our front sidewalk just kneeling like I was in church or something. I looked like a complete idiot. People would come by and ask me if I was praying or something. I would try to play it off real quick like I was pulling weeds or something. It was soooooo embarrassing.

We ended up moving out to the county from our little house in the city, which was all we had known, and there is a big difference in the two. Mom got a job at some condominiums cleaning the laundry rooms, and empty apartments, plus we were allowed to rent an apartment there. We went from food stamps, goodwill clothes, and no utilities, straight to a bunch of rich, well raised county people. We got enrolled in school there, but still had our goodwill clothes, although everyone else was dressed like Rodeo Drive. We got free lunch in a school where no one else did. We did not even have health insurance, and my mom forged out shot records to keep us in school. We did not have any furniture in our apartment. It sucked as much as our place in the city, just in a different area. I was not allowed to listen to music, or watch TV. My room had a dresser, and a bed. My sister had a room with a stereo, and a television. Heather could have friends come over, go out with friends, date, wear makeup, and even had a job. I was not allowed to do anything but go to church. I just sat in my room alone, or would go babysit any chance I got. Mom took the money I made, but I didn't care. I just wanted to get away from her and not be screamed at, and insulted and told what a useless piece of garbage I was. I hated even being alive at this point and could not understand what I had done to make God hate me so much that this was my life would pray all the time and beg God to help me not have to live in a world where I was hated. For a long time I thought he had just left me alone, and didn't answer me. But it was not Him doing these things to me, and He was the reason I was able to endure it and survive. He did not abandon me, it was God got me through it.

My mom truly hated me, and did not even bother to hide it anymore. We had one Christmas there, and she complained the whole time because she did not even want to buy me anything. What she did wrap for me was clothes and shoes in her, and my sister's size. I was way smaller, and I got a couple of books and things that really did not want me to have. After I opened everything, they took all the stuff for themselves and I got nothing. She just wanted nice presents under the tree to look good for her friends.

I got into so much trouble all the time because, I was made to feel I could never be as perfect as all the other kids at our church were. I had never had any parenting, or parents for that matter, and even now that she was "saved" she didn't teach us how to live or be or anything, I don't think she had a clue what she was doing either. She was still nuts. I was skipping school every day, because I was not allowed to go anywhere or talk to anyone, I sneaked out of church and went to smoke weed with my friends I had no self-esteem or social skills since I was never allowed around other people, or allowed to have friends. I'm lucky somebody didn't kill me or something.

Mom spent that summer visiting my dad in prison while she shipped my sister off to a preacher in California she barely knew. He had asked if Heather could come up and spend the summer with their family and go to their youth services. Mom let her go God knows why, but she didn't know those people, and the guy turned out to be a total disgusting pervert. My sister Heather gave up on any type of normal life after that. I spent that whole summer alone with mom, I followed her around doing whatever I could to make her like me, and was able to see my dad every week, which was awesome. Since my dad didn't really like my mom he arranged for her to visit one of his friends. The arrangement was, she could visit this inmate, who was a rapist, and I could visit my dad. I don't know what my parents cared about, but it didn't seem to be about us. We would go up and visit dad, but he went to bed a lot earlier than we wanted. This in turn, left me hanging around the visiting room of a men's maximum security prison by myself while mom got to know her new friend. Really, it wasn't that bad, nobody bothered me, I think they respected my dad, and felt sorry for me. So then, mom decided she is going to marry the convicted rapist as soon as he gets released. She was all happy going to visit all the time, and acted like this was a normal thing.

Soon after, my dad got transferred to another prison, and I just had to go and spend the whole time wandering around talking to inmates and guards, I don't know why she didn't just leave me at home. Seems to me it would have made more sense than letting me hang out in a men's prison. I did meet a lot of my dad's friends, but if they were being perverts, they kept it to themselves and no one was disrespectful to me. At the end of the summer Heather came back from California, of course she started coming to prison visits with us. She was 15, almost 16, but I was really immature for my age. Heather seemed more grown up, and she was very pretty. Mom had a little group of people she sat with in the room, and one of the girls was visiting my future brother-in-law who was in there for robbing a Motomart. He was 22, and Heather fell for him instantly, he got released from prison shortly after our visit. One of the inmates my mom had been socializing with in her little circle of visiting room friends, was a guy who was in for raping his 15 yr. old niece. His name was Dave, and he got released shortly after, he came over to our house one night and spent the night with my mom.

I guess because of religious reasons, or something they felt they had to get married. Mom just stopped going to visit the other guy without saying anything to the guy she had been visiting. I guess she didn't figure she would ever have to see him again so who cares? Well I was getting in trouble in school so much the principal put me in this program for bad kids. They decided to take us on a field trip to a prison to scare us straight. Yup-they took me to the very prison I had just spent my whole summer. I didn't even tell the principal I was just going along for the ride. He figured out something was going on when the bus driver got lost on the way there, and I started giving him directions. Then when we got there to the prison everybody in the place, the inmates, and guards, all of them kept coming up saying "Angel, oh my God what are you doing here??" My principal looked over at me, and asked "who are you??" Then all of a sudden, my moms inmate boyfriend she had left behind comes up, and follows me throughout my whole field trip asking me questions about why my mom just stopped coming up to see him. I had to explain to him in front of everyone from my school, and my principal. I didn't even know how to feel or act in this one. It was kind of, yeah you are from a broken home and it is o.k., but I think they thought it was a little weird-about my mom's new husband. That kind of sucked it was humiliating. It was a little funny though freaking out my principal, he did not call my house so much after that.

The next month was like a tornado at our house. Mom was married to the man she had met in the prison who was recently released for raping his 15 yr. old niece. Heather ran off with her 22 yr. old boyfriend that she had met in the prisoners visiting room whenever she got the chance and no one was looking. I was still not allowed to watch TV or listen to the stereo or have a friend over, beside that no one noticed, or cared what I did. I skipped school almost every day that year. Every time Heather would run off with Nelson I would get in trouble, because mom thought I would know where she was, and it was all so stupid. I don't know why my mom did not just find a way to give me away to someone unless, she did not know how. I did solve the problem for her, and I am sure the only thing she felt was relief.

They spent too many days and nights looking for Heather and Nelson, trying to make Heather come back home, and keeping the two of them apart. Our lives seemed to revolved around this. I'm not sure where I may have fit in their lives. It was like Angel who? Many parents might say that I needed some help with school, or perhaps some counseling, but for real, I felt like I was nothing but a burden in the house, and had been since the day I was born. For some reason they just didn't ever care what I did or what became of me.

Sometimes when Heather, and Nelson would go out they would take me with them so I could get out of the house I suppose. I didn't care why, I just loved hanging out with them. They both felt like parents to me somehow. Heather had always been the only mother figure

I had known, so when she got with Nelson he just kind of got thrown in there with her. He tried to stick up for me with my mom sometimes, and tell her she was being horrid to me, and I do appreciate that, of course didn't listen. They wanted to go out one night and dropped me off at a Steak and Shake and left me there for eight hours I sat there talking to all the people that come in and out in the middle of the night. Most of them were truckers, but a couple were real weirdo's., I am so lucky I never got stolen, as I was a kidnappers dream. No one would have even noticed or cared if I was gone. When they finally came back to pick me up in the morning, I was so mad at Heather that we got into a fight in the Steak and Shake parking lot. They dropped me back off at home and I wondered if they ever gave a thought to what I went through while they were out doing whatever they did?

Every time Heather and Nelson took off somewhere I got the crap beat out of me with whatever was handy, because my mom and her newest husband were convinced I knew where she was. Heather had taken off to my grandma's house way out in the country on one occasion. My mom became convinced I had some extra information on the way up there, so here I am stuck in the front seat by her when she reaches over and slaps me across my face, then pulled the car over, and told me to get out in the middle of nowhere. She drove off and then came back a few minutes later and I got beat all the way home because all I did was cross over the highway and stick my thumb out. I hitchhiked all the time, so I really didn't care so much about being left. I learned young because, I had no choice but to find a way to survive. Yes, it hurt really bad to know that my mother truly hated me, and at this point in my life I didn't even understand why know I just assumed that it was because I was disgusting and unlovable. Sometimes she would get so disgusted with me she would make me go out and sleep in the yard. I missed my dad and wanted him to rescue me so bad that is all I ever thought about. It is what got me through all of the horrible, sad, lonely moments that were my childhood spent every day skipping school to hang out with the few friends I did have. It was too hard to explain why I was not allowed to talk on the phone or go anywhere, so I just didn't talk to very many people. By this point I didn't really care about anything. I got beat no matter what I did so I did not even bother trying. At night we would go to the church, mom and her husband would sit there and try to look normal, I was sometimes amazed how my mom would get herself all dressed up, grab the biggest bible she could carry, sit there through an entire church service, then come home and treat her own child like a dog. I will never understand why I didn't get to go anywhere, or have anyone come to my home. I was so freaking sad, and Heather, of course was off with Nelson somewhere. Right around my 15th birthday, Heather and Nelson were gone so much, my mom decided one night that I knew where they were again wasn't even allowed out of the house, or use a telephone, so I'm not sure how I was supposed to be getting all this inside information. I guess blaming me, made more sense than admitting she shouldn't have taken her teenage daughter to a men's prison, and then allowed male inmates to stay at our house after they were released.

All of our lives were so completely out of control. Mom came and told me that she believed I knew where Heather had went. I really didn't know. Mom's newest husband of 3 weeks, newly released from prison for violently raping his own brothers 15 yr. old daughter—felt it was his duty as man of the house, to, "spank me" so he threw me face first into the living room stereo, cutting my left eyelid open where I still have a mark. I had large handprint bruises all around my neck, deep purple whelps and bruises in the shape of the belt he had used on me all over my arms and covering my legs. Cuts on the back of my leg, and I had barely recovered from a cyst on my tailbone causing me to not even be able to walk, without a large amount of pain, from this "spanking, all because my sister had ran away from home, and they wanted me to tell them where she was. I really did not know, as God is my witness to this day, I did not know where she was, but I did get the crap beat out of me that day anyway, and then those people went to bed and slept like babies.

My mom had a traffic ticket she had not paid, and a bench warrant had been issued for her arrest. My mom's sister called and had the police pick my mom up for the traffic warrant, then Heather called, and asked me what had happened. I told her, and the next few hours were a terrifying ordeal. It was a minute by minute pulse pounding terrifying experience. Was my mom ever coming home? My Aunt Shirley had been the one to call the police to arrest my mom, and send DCFS to our door. Mom kept calling every two minutes for me to call my aunt to get her out of jail was by myself in the house and my aunt and my sister told me they were going to send help. My mom is at the police station where she was handcuffed to a wall wanting me to call her sister to get her out. Little did she know that her sister was the one who had them come and pick her up and was trying to get me removed from the house? DCFS finally showed up to look at me and ask me questions. I was so scared my mom was going to come in and catch me talking to them. I'm not sure what I thought she would do, but I was so terrified. I didn't think anybody was really going to get me out of there. Mom stayed in the slammer until after we were gone and I made it out eventually.

The DCFS people took me to St. Ann Police Department, and took pictures of all my injuries, and left me in emergency foster care. After that I spent 2 months in an orphanage. At the time, it was a large old building full of kids people had treated badly, or didn't want. I don't think I felt sad about it, but it hurt that my mom never even asked how I was, or tried to get me back. Apparently she was relieved that I was gone. All the other kids had parents who came to visit them and brought them things. They were making all sorts of efforts to get them back. I just sat there like some old discarded garbage. My mom never showed up for court, and said she didn't know how I got those injuries. She then moved with no forwarding address. Can one even imagine how I felt sitting there in that home alone and unwanted?

The home had six girls, and six boys. We spent our days cleaning the place, cooking meals, and doing our laundry. They let us have bus passes to go to the zoo and stuff. It really was kind of cool, but if I had ever known what it felt like to have a parent love me or want me that would have been horrible. For me however, it wasn't and that in itself is really sad. The final result of that was being placed in foster care for two years.

I think that may have been the most, "normal," time I had as a child. I played soccer and softball, was on the honor roll, went to homecoming, had friends, even dated one of the cutest guys in school all through high school. I was, of course, a foster kid and that never went away. The family I lived with was really nice at the time, and I am sure they tried very hard to make me feel part of the family, but I did get treated like a "foster kid". I won't pretend like I didn't. How do I even describe that? It is kind of like using food stamps or getting free lunch but at home. You feel inferior, less than, just not as good as everyone else at the table. Everyone pretended like it was a whole family, but one know it's not. In Family pictures, they take 2 shots, one with you in it, one without you, just in case you're temporal.

I had a good time, I laughed and was happy. I got to be a normal teenager, if there is such a thing. Heather got pregnant with her oldest son, and her and Nelson got married on her 17th birthday had some problems from being so emotionally battered, they tried to put me into therapy and I ended up in the nuthouse a couple times. I had begun cutting my arms a little bit, but for the most part I was good. Right before I turned 18, they gave me up one day because, they said I got in a fight with my foster brother. He whined about it, and I had to move. I ended up back at my mom's house. Foster parents don't keep the kids if they are not getting paid anyway, but it was nice while it lasted. I only went back to my mom's because my sister was living there again since her husband was in prison.

Her husband, Nelson had violated his parole, and had to complete his sentence. She had 2 young boys by this time. She was actually pregnant with their youngest when I first got there. They were so adorable I loved them little critters so much. They were the reason I stayed the 6 months. She got a divorce and I guess they both moved in different directions, didn't see Nelson again for many years and found him again in in think 2005 He is taking good care of my nephew still and is still an important part of my life. He is still my big brother. I stayed about 6 more months, mom and creep dad wasn't allowed to hit me anymore, but it still sucked. Those people just never even mentioned my being in foster care, or taken away, much less said they were sorry. While I was gone they told people from the church that I was incorrigible and they had to put me into some type of institution. I left high school because it was hard enough to live in the same house with my mom all I did was get berated and emotionally abused. I could not go to high school and be locked back in my room again like that. I still was not allowed to listen to music or watch TV or use the phone or have any type of friends. I was almost 18 and had been allowed these things at the foster family, so I could not go back to that life again. I quit school, and got a job at a restaurant. **AND THEN MY ENTIRE LIFE CHANGED**.

One day as I was working the register, at lunch rush, busy as hell, I looked up, and there is, my dad, standing in line. I did not even know he had been released from prison. He just smiled at me and I was in shock so bad, I didn't know what to think. I broke the cash register, and had to call the manager over to fix it because I had pushed so many buttons when I saw him. I had waited 18 years in utter misery, and sadness for this man to come and rescue me from this person who hated me, and-here he finally was. I sat down and talked to him, but all I wanted to know was, "when are you coming to get me?" He was so freaked out about my desperation, he thought I was in some kind of trouble. I told him no, I've just been waiting my whole life to be with my dad and I love you. He was still living in a halfway house at the time and couldn't rescue me quite yet. I could not let my mom know he was coming up to see me all the time. So I spent every shift juggling my dad and my stepdad, and it was a little nerve racking. I had to ride the bus to work every day, and dad was working at a trucking agency He would stop by in the afternoon and I would make him lunch, and we would talk. I was so happy and so excited, as it was the first time in my entire life I had a parent that loved me and wanted me. I was," **Somebody's Daughter**, "that was a wonderful feeling I had never felt before. I made him promise me the second he got out he would come and get me, and so he came to visit me at work for 2 months. I was still technically a legal ward of the state, because of my mom's abuse, and having been in foster care. I have to sneak lunch with my dad, but my mom never knew he was there.

May 9th, 1986 around 1 a.m. my dad and I executed my escape. He came up to work that afternoon and cashed my paycheck for me. My stepdad usually did this for me so I had to lie about that when I got home. Then I had to wait until mom and Dave went to sleep. Lying in bed a nervous wreck just waiting. Then up to pack my stuff, and wait. We had it planned that I would meet him 2 blocks from my house I waited until 1 a.m. when we were supposed to meet up. He of course was drunk, and had just been released from a halfway house. After being paroled for murder charges, and the first stop he had made was the bar, and then to bust me out, and take me home.

Suddenly, we hear nonstop police sirens. I think it's him, and he thinks it's for me. It wasn't either one of us, and I grabbed a bag of shit, and ran down the road and got in his car. I had escaped. Finally, after waiting, literally my entire life, my dad had come to rescue me. He drove me down to North St. Louis and we were home. I had never been so happy in my life. All I had wanted since I was too young to talk was to be with my dad. I never cared what he had done, or where he had been forgave any mistake he ever made. I just wanted to be by my daddy and I finally got him. We talked about everything, he never sugar coated anything he told me who, and what was fucked up. He would go to take a nap, and I would go and snuggle up by him, and talk his ear off instead. I knew I had 3 other sisters but had not gotten to be around them much, we were in different places doing different things, of course, and my mom wouldn't let me go around them. The first one I just got to be so close to was my sister Rose. We shared a room together from day one as far as I remembered. We did not know each other but we just clicked. We spent every waking moment together. I will admit I was a terrible influence on the poor girl. She is 3 years younger than me. However, she did give me lots of side ideas in our crimes, and was a total willing participant. We stole my dad's car every night, we bought liquor, and got drunk in Hyde Park and smoked weed. We had curfews, but our dad could not catch us sneaking out of the house our room was on the top floor of the house and the door to the back steps was in our room. We would come in on time, kiss everyone good night, and then bolt out that backdoor. We were involved in some badass drag races down 9th street, one puppy theft, numerous grand theft auto expeditions, and we would stay out partying all night, then sneak back in the back door and climb in our big double bed we shared like a couple of little angels kind of got caught one night cause, we went to a party at my friend Teds house, and I drank a whole 5th of Peach Schnapps, and got arrested. Rose had snuck home and got herself back in bed and never even got caught. She was so much slicker than me, but we sure did have a lot of fun. Dad and my stepmom were a little suspicious so they put nails on the door to keep it shut. They put them on the inside and bent em over, we just bent the nails back and slipped out anyway. Then dad went through our dresser drawer and found the copies of his car keys we had made. I think I got grounded for, like a week or something. We had so much fun.

I followed my dad around like a happy little puppy. My whole, empty, hurting, traumatized heart was finally made complete. He was all I ever wanted, my dad was my hero. He had black curly hair and blue eyes that looked like cold steel when he was mad. Big strong arms that felt soft too when he hugged me, and he told me he loved me all the time. He was so freakin cool, he didn't care what anyone thought about anything, and everyone I knew was scared of him. He was so freakin cool. My sister Renee was 15 when I moved down to North St. Louis, she was 6 months pregnant with my nephew and we didn't get to hang out much then, but that came later. She was such a mother hen even then always yelling at me and Rose. Our youngest sister Penny was 8 when I moved down there with them. She was so little and so much younger than us. I took her with me a couple times on dates but I sure do wish we could have been closer. My dad, I found out after I moved in, was a pretty violent drunk. Once I wasn't there but my stepmom came downstairs and her whole face was beat the hell up, she said my dad had done it. I didn't even know what to think I was so shocked. I asked him later why he did that, he did not really explain very much to me, maybe he was just crazy I guess. All he told me was he hated when he did shit like that because he felt bad later, and it made his hands hurt. One day I was there when my stepmom, Annie had come home from work and we stayed a little late because our boss got a keg of beer for everybody, and we celebrated our profit sharing checks. I guess Annie knew he was going to be mad already because she told me she was going to sneak down in the basement, and not to tell him where she was. So I went in and he asked of course, where did Annie go?? I just kept telling him I didn't know. He hit me once in the mouth, and busted my lip open, also my head flew back and cracked the back of it on the doorframe. He hit me a couple times, and I never would say where she was. She peeked in the kitchen window, and saw him hit me so she came in so he would stop. My dad started beating the hell out of her, and my little baby sister Penny was there. I just grabbed her and we went up to the gas station a few blocks away, I guess I freaked out, and didn't really know what to do.

I called the police from the gas station, and told them my dad was beating the hell out of my mom, I was so afraid for her. I bought Penny a little pack of cookies and we went back home. BY this point he had beat her beyond recognition and stuffed her in a closet. All the sudden the police showed up and dad told them he did not give permission for them to come in. I yelled out from behind him, I live here too and I do give you permission; my mom needs help. I was brave there, and did not even realize it at the time. Police came in and arrested him for assault on both of us. Paramedics came and took care of Annie and took her to the hospital. Poor little 8 year old Penny watched the whole thing. Dad got out of jail that same night, even though he was on parole for murder, they never did anything about the assault charges. He was so mad at me for a while, after that he couldn't believe I called the police on him. I can't believe I did either. I was never sorry for that though. We made up, of course. He did not hit her again after that. Dad and I ended up moving out, and taking my little sister Penny with us. Dad was driving a truck over the road and I was working in a factory. I had to work a lot so I got her a babysitter before, and after work. Dad only got to come home 2 nights a week, and I would fry him up a whole chicken to take back out with him to eat on the road. I had Penny like that for about a year. The little Monkeyhead.

Since I was only 18 and had not been allowed to date, my dad gave me a curfew and said, "You can date someone if they come home to meet me, and I approve of them." When I told young men this, they said yeah we don't want to take you out that bad, your dads a big old boy. I did finally get to date, and then I ended up getting married when I was 19. I had my first son when I was 20. I named him Luke after my husband, but he ended up being nicknamed Bug, and that name stuck with him his entire life. I have never called him anything different. That got started when his dad said he looked like a little Bug crawling around on the floor, and it stuck because he was a human tornado when he was little and, bugged the crap out of everyone. I thought he was perfect and still do. He was really cute, of course and very funny and smart use to go everywhere with him and just thought I had given birth to the most handsome amazing baby ever in the world. My brother in law, Lee use to make fun of him because it would make me so mad. I would get really mad if I didn't feel people were appreciating the wondrousness of Bug.

My dad **HATE**, **HATE**, **HATED** my first husband, he never pretended different and never got over it. We were married for about 2 years. I was so young when we got married and had never even known any couples that were happy, and lived a normal life to know what it was supposed to be like, I was 19 yrs. old and we moved to a different state to be near my husband's family. Of course I did not know anyone there, and we were broke as hell, because I had lost my job and couldn't find another one being pregnant. We could not afford for me to drive to Missouri where my entire family lived, and there was no free long distance then, it was so very expensive. My husband didn't know what he was doing either. He barely spoke to me, and complained about working all the time just to pay bills. I was so lonely and miserable. I packed up finally and moved out on our first anniversary. I went back to St Louis and got a job at a towing company where my sister Rose worked. I only stayed gone for a few weeks until he talked me into coming back home. I still never got over the way he had acted when I was pregnant. He could go out and hang with his friends, and go drinking and do God knows what, but I just sat in the house bored. I love him to death now, but back then he was kind of a jerk to me. He didn't want to be in the house with a wife and be married, clearly. I had no one to talk to but the walls, and I was lonely as hell, and mad as shit from the way he treated me the whole time I was pregnant.

After I had been free for a while, I was really unhappy and did not want to be cooped up in the house with him anymore. I did not even really like him by this point. He had ignored me for two freakin years. So I turned 21 and went buck wild. I would go to the bar every chance I got, and didn't come home anytime I was supposed to. I guess I kind of acted like he did when I was pregnant with BUG, I wrecked both of our cars, and we fought nonstop of course. He got arrested 2 times for battery because of the fights we had. But I hit him too, maybe not on those days but I'd say we were equal assholes to each other. I can't say I was battered there at all, we just fought. I wanted to move out and just get away, but he did not want me to go, and said if I would just stay I could do whatever I wanted to do. So he worked 1st shift, and I worked 2nd shift. We took turns taking care of Bug who was only a year old. It didn't really work out very well. I ended up moving for good after we had been married 2 yrs. I just couldn't do it anymore. Neither one of us treated the other one good at all, nor did we have a clue how to make a marriage work. I have no ill feelings toward him whatsoever I love him very much now. He's part of our family now that were all grown up and living separately.

I think I was 22 when I met Steve Parker, he was young and I was young, so we dated for a while and I realized I was pregnant with my daughter. I didn't trust him to be around. He was immature and we broke up when I was 3 weeks pregnant. I was working at a pizza restaurant, and I met Donnie Novak. He kept coming up to my job and asking me to go out with him.

I kept telling him no because I had too much stuff going on, but he would not give up. I kept telling him it was not a good time, and he would wait outside my job, come to my house, but he was so cool; all James Dean-ish. I just wanted to move back to St. Louis and start over, but he said nope, were going to do this thing, and I want to be there for you and these kids. I was so young, so naive, and he lied so well.

I was less than 2 months pregnant with Amanda and standing in the living room one day, holding Bug who wasn't 2 yet. I don't think so anyway. Donnie came home drunk, he had been out driving on the road he said doing some work with his Uncle Calvin. I never even expected it but, he yelled at me, and slapped me really hard right in my face. I was so shocked, I just walked out the door with Bug and, went to the only place close, the restaurant I worked at. I didn't even know what to do or say. He had slapped me across the side of my face in front of his brother, and cousin and a friend, and no one said a word, so I walked out. I was embarrassed, and a couple of my friends were sitting on the front porch of the restaurant, but I didn't tell anyone he had hit me. He came right behind me and scared off all my friends, and I don't know what happened, he said he wouldn't do it again. I was so young, so confused, and so gullible. I stayed and I worked full time, and had Bug full time. The baby would come to work with me sometimes, because his dad would come up and drop him off there in the middle of my shift. I finally got fired when I was about 4 months pregnant, because Luke dropped Bug off at the restaurant in the middle of dinner rush, and Bug broke more stuff than my boss felt like dealing with. I really don't know what to do at this point I guess.

My family did not know Donnie hits me, I'm not sure why I didn't tell them. I felt shame and thought I deserved to be treated like that. If I had called my dad, he would have driven all the way down to Collinsville, Illinois and killed him. I had several very large uncles and cousins. I never said a word. I guess I thought they would blame me, or act like it was no big deal, I had seen my dad hit his wives and maybe it was ok. I just didn't think anyone would protect me. Donnie had gotten to where he was disappearing all the time to go out drinking and coming home drunk, and calling me terrible names telling me how much he hated me, and beating the crap out of me. He would come home some nights and hit me or kick me while I was sleeping pregnant, or not he didn't care. I was scared but I also just felt like that's what I deserved. Most likely because, of the way I was raised with my mom telling me I was worthless and then hitting me like that, I just really didn't know what was right or wrong anymore. I can never get the image of his face looking all angry and hateful over my head with his hand raised to hit me while he was screaming at me. I hate it but that is the face I will always remember.

We moved to St. Louis, and my sister, and brother—in—law lived in the same apartment complex. Heather had divorced Nelson by now, and remarried her second husband, Lee Meuller who was an awesome brother to me. I still hadn't said a word to anyone about how

Donnie treated me. It was such a shitty life being big and pregnant when I should have been happy about it, and with someone else who was happy about it also. But the bigger I got the more he resented Steve Parker, and the worse he treated me. His dad was a diabetic, and very sick from time to time. Every time his dad got real bad off Donnie would get drunk on whiskey, and beat the crap out of me. He was nice to everybody else though. They all thought he was the greatest guy in the world. One night when I was 7 months pregnant with Amanda, Donnie came home and broke my nose.(that freakin hurt). Bug was 2 and sleeping in the next room. As soon as Donnie hit me I snuck into get Bug so we could get out, and I heard Donnie cocking a shotgun. So I am 7 months pregnant, with a broken nose, dragging a sleeping 2 yr. old very quietly out of our house because, I didn't know which person he was going shoot, and didn't want to find out.

I went over to Heathers, and she called my mom, who knew a judge. The next afternoon I went back home by myself, and calmly started packing Donnie's clothes in a box while he was in the other room.

He heard a knock on the door, and when he answered it the sheriff told him you don't live here anymore. I handed him his box of clothes, and he left. Damn he was mad though. He had hit me a lot when I was pregnant with Amanda. There's no way to explain why I was so scared to leave. Everyone who tried to help me got hurt, and I was scared and humiliated. I was in the hospital a lot during that pregnancy, and I just always said he didn't do anything when the police would ask me how I got hurt. They didn't believe me, but couldn't ever prove he did it.

Right, after I had my daughter, Amanda Grace Novak, she was just a few days old, and my brother—in—law watched the kids while we went to the store. Donnie got mad at me while he was driving, stopped the car got out and threw the whole set of keys at my head. Have you ever been hit in the head with a whole set of keys?? It gave me puncture wounds on the top of my head, bleeding down my face like a stuck pig, he got arrested on the side of the road. Police drove me home and I just walked in my house and calmly told Lee he could stop babysitting now because I was home. He started to get up and go in the other room, happened to glance at my face covered in blood and said "what the hell happened to you??" He took everything Donnie owned and threw it in the yard and slept by my front door on the floor all night. I stayed by myself with the kids for a while, but then Bug got **REALLY** sick for a couple weeks. I couldn't get him to the doctor or do all, to care for him as bad as he was. Donnie came back and took care of Bug and just kind of stayed. I was grateful he was taking care of my son when he was so sick, and he was being nice. I was young and dumb, and had Battered Woman Syndrome, rather I knew it or not. Not surprisingly, Donnie started hitting me more, and more, and was beating the crap out of me in public constantly. He didn't care who saw it, and almost everyone was scared of him, I couldn't go to the bathroom any place we went too, when he got mad he would come in there and kick the door in and beat the crap out of me. He would get thrown out of every restaurant or bar we went in, and didn't care he would just wait in the parking lot for me to finally come out, I couldn't hide in there forever.

Everyone was scared to help me except for our cousin Jimmy Novak. He was the only person who ever saw him hit me that told him he was wrong. He was so mean, and loud, and scary. I will never forget the way he looked when he punched me in my face, and I didn't know why he was screaming at me of how much he hated me. But he wouldn't let me leave. We would go out with all his friends and as soon as he got real drunk he would talk about me like a dog, and I would just have to sit there and listen to it. If I tried to leave he would beat me up in front of everyone. He would tell his family that I hit him first, and he was defending himself or I was just crazy.

All his friends knew me as the crazy bitch who had him arrested all the time for no reason. I couldn't tell anyone any different because, they knew him better than they did me. They were his friends, and I was scared, and didn't know what to do. I wasn't hitting him, and the only thing crazy about me back then was that I stayed with him. I did get really tired of it at one point, and couldn't take it anymore Waiting all night for him to come home, getting beaten and treated like shit when he did get home, being openly cheated on constantly just couldn't deal with it somehow, and I had to get away from him. I left him for 6 months when Amanda was a baby and Bug was 3, I felt so good when I was there and glad not to have to deal with all of his crazy stuff. I didn't plan very well, or think enough about what I was going to do with myself. I did not do all that great back in St. Louis so I stayed with my sister, and brother in law. I started dating an old friend of mine, and he was not all that great to me either. I'm not sure why I attract these kinds of people, but I do. New guy ended up being a creep too and hit me several times, then slept with my sister. I called Donnie and had him come to pick me up. I did not know what the hell to do at this point.

Shortly after we got back together I found out I was pregnant with Donnie Jr., my youngest son. Donnie immediately remembered that he hated me. I had more black eyes during that pregnancy than well, anyone should have ever. Amanda was a baby, and did not really know what was going on. Bug was old enough to know his mom was getting hit a lot. He would cry, and throw stuff at Donnie. He went through a lot of trauma because of it and, I am so sorry he had to go through that. I did not realize at the time the effect domestic violence has on children who witness it. I just assumed that since he wasn't the one getting hit he would be okay really have no excuse for making him go through that except I didn't know how to get out of it. Every single time before that I had told the police he did not hit me, but when I was 8 months pregnant with Donnie Jr. he gave me a black eye and hit me with my car. I went straight to Collinsville's police station, and filled out a report. I told him after that every single time he hit me I was going to call the police, because I didn't know what else to do and so, I did. We moved to Maryville when I was pregnant with Donnie Jr., but Donnie rarely worked, and when he did he kept all the money he made to spend at the bar. He never brought it home and paid the bills with it, or prepare for our sons upcoming birth. We did not even have so much as a pack of diapers. I don't know how we thought we were going to take care of this baby. The police in Collinsville, got so tired of seeing me covered in blood with black eyes. Every time Donnie went anywhere they stopped him and held him as long as they could while they berated him for being an abusive husband, father and a bully. All our neighbors hated him. While I was pregnant I signed up for GED classes so I could take the test. I had been out of school for a while and Donnie hated me going back to school. He did whatever he could to keep me from getting to my classes.

I skipped a lot of classes because of black eyes or sometimes because I was embarrassed. I was very pregnant with a black eye and could not look anyone in the eye. Nobody wants to talk to someone like that, and he thought he was winning. When the day came for me to take the test I drove up to that school and took it anyway just out of stubbornness to prove he did not beat me down, and that I could do it. I was in labor with Donnie Jr. during the whole test, and had to keep going out into the hall to take breaks when I was having contractions. I did finish it, and I passed that test. When I went into labor in the middle of the night he packed up Bug and Amanda and drove up to the hospital. He dropped me off alone at the emergency to deliver our child by myself. He never came back to be there for the delivery. I had so much trouble, and Donnie Jr. stopped breathing, and his heart slowed down so they performed an emergency C-section. Then I had a seizure, and we both ended up having to stay in the hospital for 5 days instead of the planned 24 hours. My foster mom came up to see me and dropped off a whole supply of every single thing I could need to bring a baby home at my house. Then when they had the steak dinner for the parents he didn't show up. And when I got released from the hospital with our son, I couldn't find Donnie Novak. I sat there in the room discharged with a newborn baby for 6 hours calling every bar in town to have him give us a ride home.

He didn't even wait until I got the stitches out of my stomach from the C-section before he threw me against a kitchen counter and hurt my back, ripped my stitches and left. He was beating me so badly so often, all of our new neighbors called the police every time they heard a sound, and it was always me with not just a small bruise. No woman should ever have her face beaten like that. I am still ashamed it happened to me and hurt to think about it

We finally had to move out of that town also because the police hated him so bad. I tried to keep taking care of the kids, and keep a normal household, but it was so hard. I never knew when I was going to get beat up in front of my kids. If he was going to help me pay our bills, and 98% of the time he did not. But when I had to go to Bugs preschool with a big black eye and trying to act like I didn't notice it to make holiday t-shirts everyone made me feel bad, they just wouldn't look at me or talk to me, only whispered about me, I know they knew why I looked like that. I just kept my head down, and only talked to Bug while we did his project He didn't think anything of the way I looked so I made it fun for him I'm sure they all had something to say, but what was I going to do?

It kept getting harder and harder. My dad still did not know of my abuse. Heather and Lee knew it had happened in the past, but they were heroin addicts and didn't check up on it. Caseyville police were at our house damn near every day, when Donnie's dad died he came home and beat my entire face in. I was covered in blood and had 3 small kids in bed, grabbed them and threw them in my car and tried to just drive away. Five cop cars surrounded my car before I even made it out the driveway. The neighbors had called, and they thought it was him in the car trying to leave. Beat up, and my face bleeding, I got out and of course they put me to the side. We had an old man next door called the police every time I screamed. They took pictures of me, I asked them not to arrest him because his dad's funeral was the next day. They charged him with domestic battery and I left with the kids to go stay at my sister's house in St. Louis. I have a 4 yr. old, 2 yr. old, and maybe 4 month old baby. I made it as far as East St. Louis on the highway, my radiator leaks, and my car breaks down. It's about 2:00 a.m. luckily emergency road service shows up, fixes my car and told me he could see that I looked like I running from something because I still had blood all over me. The car wasn't going to make it any further. Some guy stopped and offered us a ride back home. I put the kids in his car, since I really had no choice, and a garbage truck stopped too and followed us back to my house I waited while this guy carried my 3 kids back in my house to make sure he was trying anything weird. We had to climb over the broken storm door lying across the living room doorway that Donnie had kicked in earlier. After the man left I went in my room to try and sleep, to find Donnie had already been bonded out, and was asleep in our bed. I was so scared I knew he was going to be mad at me, because he had gotten arrested. Boy was I right he was mad. I lost my job because I could not go to work without looking all beaten up, or being too hurt to even go.

We packed up the kids in a U-Haul and moved up to Kansas City, MO, where my dad lived. I guess I was 25. We could not make it on our own at that time because, Donnie either, didn't work or didn't ever bring his paycheck home for bills. So we moved into a vacant house my dad owned and Donnie didn't hit me the whole time we were in Kansas City. He didn't work, or pay bills and pretty well disgusted my dad. My dad was a hard worker and couldn't stand lazy people. I can't believe Donnie wasn't at least shamed into working, and supporting his family. My dad never sugar coated anything or hid how he felt about him just lying around not doing shit. My dad even bought Donnie a lawn mower and brought it over to our house, told him to go cut grass or something but quit being a bum, and support your family. It didn't do any good. It wasn't a real bad time there. I got to see my dad all the time, and he was around the kids, I loved that and he was over at our house all the time, and just hanging out He use to take Bug fishing with him, and bring him back home dressed exactly like he was; that was so funny. Amanda and Donnie Jr. were pretty small still, Bug was a little older and he really had some good times there. I use to get up around six in the mornings, probably because that is when Bug got up. I would start getting my laundry washed, and hanging out on the clothesline with my little Bug following me around, he would have me out there in the yard playing baseball with him at the crack of dawn, playing in the dirt with him like I was a little kid. He was so cool. We spent a lot of time together. Kansas City is kind of, a hoosier town, where I lived anyway. People would put living room furniture on their porches and just sit out on it like it was normal. A lot of people had yard sales everyday as a job. Just sitting on their porches, on their couch, selling crap. There were thrift stores on every corner, I use to love going to the thrift stores with my dad, and the kids. My dad was so cheap, so I finally figured out where I got it from. He was getting the kids, having them spend the night over with him, and getting to know them, I was pretty happy. Everything I wanted was finally here and Donnie and I, didn't have much money but we were ok. I grew up with no money at all so it didn't bother me as much as it should have. We had all kind of friends, a couple neighbors across the alley, and some next door. My dad, and his girlfriend at the time, whose name was Jolene, had been married to my dad's brother a long time ago, and two of her kids were my cousins, we were just having fun. There was always someone coming or going at my house. On most weekends everyone gathered at my house. I'm not really sure how I started being suspicious about Donnie doing drugs. He just disappeared mysteriously, and had marks on his arms. I just felt like something wasn't right. I started watching him more, but never could really prove anything, but I was young, and naive, and really didn't know what I was looking for.

If he would have started painting all over our house, or was going up and down the alley with our laundry throughout the night, I would have figured it out sooner, but I was kind of living in a fool's paradise. He wasn't gone at the bar all the time, he wasn't hitting me, and I was spending all of my time with my family. It really was better than it had been before. At this point in my life I was **THE** most against drugs person you could ever meet. I didn't like what I saw my sister and brother—in—law, and their kids going through. I didn't like how it made my mom act. Suddenly, it seemed that my whole world just completely blew up in my face. I felt my entire life and been ripped to shreds, and scattered with no warning, never to be the same again.

First, my dad came over to my house one night very upset, and told me Jolene had disappeared the night before, and slept with his brother. He was very upset and told me he was going to move out that Friday when he got paid. I don't think I had ever seen him look sad before. Mad yeah, but sad . . . . not so much. He told me he was going to go home and stay for a couple days, and told me he loved me and left. It was August, 9th, 1994 @ 8:10 p.m. It was a Tuesday night, I was watching Roseanne on the TV. I was wearing some cutoff Levi shorts, an aqua blue half shirt, and no shoes. I was sitting on our couch, watching my favorite show, when all of a sudden two of our neighbors beat on our door. They told Donnie to come outside, and told me to wait inside. I knew something was going on, but never in my wildest dreams did I imagine what he was about to tell me. A couple minutes later, my husband told me to come out, the neighbors were gone. Donnie sat me down on the front steps and told me my dad had overdosed on drugs. I had no idea my dad did drugs. I thought he was trying to tell me my dad committed suicide. He told me my cousin Josh was on his way to get me and take me to the hospital to see him. Josh takes me there telling me the whole way my dad is going to be ok. When I walked into the hospital my entire family is standing in the hallway waiting for me. I knew, of course, at this point my dad was gone. A nurse came to get me, and let me go and tell my dad good bye. I walked out of that hospital in a daze with a piece of my soul missing. I would never be that same person again as I was before my daddy left me for good.

The last thing he had told me as he walked out my door was," bye baby girl, I love you." A couple relatives took me with them afterwards, so we could call and notify family members from out of town. My dads' girlfriend, Jolene was sitting in the back seat with me, the brother she had slept with, and his girlfriend were in the front. I was really mad as hell at both of them, and I was not sure if my uncle's girlfriend knew about what they had done. I didn't want to add to the drama, and really didn't know what to do at this point, so I didn't say anything. I am just kind of looking out the window deep in shock.

I heard them ask Jolene if he had done more drugs that day than he usually did. All of a sudden my brain felt like a record when one suddenly jerks the needle off it, and it pulled me back into reality. I said," what do you mean more than he usually does." I had been told he committed suicide, and was mind blown over that. Now I am finding out there's something else fucked up to add to the story. They continue the conversation to the point where I find out during this car ride from hell that he died from an accidental heroin overdose. So now, I am **REALLY** against drugs, and overwhelmed with confusion. It didn't really sink in at first, that the person I had waited for all my life was really gone forever.

I made the funeral arrangements, bought clothes, ordered flowers and then I had to call my sister Rose, and ask her leave work, and go tell our grandmother her son was gone. I am sure she did not want to go do this at all, but we all needed her. I did not have a phone number for Heather to let her know our dad had died, so I had to call my mom. I asked if she would let Heather know. She tried to wait a few days to tell her until she thought it would be too late for Heather to make it to the funeral. I wired Heather 100 bucks, and she did get to take the train up to Kansas City, and attend out father's funeral. My in-laws got all 3 of my kids, and kept them for us for at least a week. During this whole time, I don't tell **ANYONE**, about my dad's girlfriend was sleeping with his brother the night before he died. I did not want them to hurt the way that I did, knowing how he spent his last night on earth, sad, and hurt. I am sure I truly hated her at that point. She went with me to the funeral home making arrangements, and clutching my dad's life insurance binder to her chest, crying in bereavement. I was the sole beneficiary so the people from the funeral home took it out of her hands and handed it to me.

My uncle tried to get the funeral home to give him a receipt for the funeral for tax purposes or whatever, but the people knew I was paying for it, so they gave him a receipt that was made out to me. Relatives came from all over the place, and went through my entire house because he had a lot of stuff there. They, tore the place apart getting mementos. They walked away leaving everything in a pile of what they did not want, and left the rest for me to clean up. Since he had left his life insurance to me, and no one else, there was a little pissiness in the air. Jolene kept his car, and everything else he owned, I could have taken it all, but I was just too hurt and messed up in the head to do anything. I wish my sisters had been closer, and we could have dealt with all of it together, but I don't think anyone knew what to do. They had to get back to work and their lives. I think Rose stayed with me for a week. She was the only person I really had to lean on. We didn't really say out loud to each other how we felt, but we held each other's hands, and made it through the hell together, that was our father's funeral. I did tell Rose later, what Jolene had done to dad, since she was the only person I could bring myself to tell. My sister Renee had three kids, and a husband back in Illinois, she wasn't able to stay, and of course I understand that. My sister Penny was still in high school, and of course she could not stay. My dad had a house, household stuff, car, a truck, and motorcycle. He had not left any of those things to me specifically. I don't know if people thought I got everything because he left the life insurance to me, but nobody except my grandpa took any of that stuff. I ended up selling his house for the back taxes to be paid, and my dad's best friend stole his truck. Jolene kept his car and all his household stuff. I was too crazy to go get it back from her, and everybody else just left me there.

Donnie was not there for me at all during this time, after all I had went through the year before when his dad died. He was busy though, doing drugs, and stealing things from my dad's house to sell and buy the drugs. Friends came and told me he sold my dad's guns, tools, all kinds of stuff, and they were gone. Finally I had enough and told him I didn't want him there. I was so freakin mentally unstable though I couldn't tell reality from a hole in the ground. Some days I was not even sure if my dad had really died, and I had to ask people if it was real. I would ask "did my dad die?", because I was not sure. I was not capable of caring for my kids in that turbulent time. I stayed in bed not sure what was going on around me. I called Bugs dad, and told him I needed help, that he needed to take him for a while. I really could not function. Bug was supposed to be starting kindergarten, and I couldn't even get out of bed. Luke came and stayed the night, and took Bug back to Illinois with him. He told me I had to sign papers for him to enroll him in school since I had sole custody. I signed the papers he brought with him and he left with Bug. I will never forget that day as I stood outside, watching the car drive away with my small

little boy, and it fading in the distance. Another little piece of me was gone. I cared more about what was best for him at that moment, than I did about my heart breaking a little bit more. He did not know what was going on that day, and just thought he was going to visit his dad He will never know how much it hurt me to do what I knew was best for him at that time. I just wanted him to be o.k., and I knew his dad would do better than I could at that time. Shortly after, I realized the papers I signed were custody papers, and not even legal, but I will get back to that later.

Donnie only stayed gone three weeks. I didn't really want him to come back, but I was a freakin vegetable at this point. I found out that my dad, his girlfriend, my cousin, our friends, and my husband were all heroin addicts. I felt stupid and disgusted, hurt, let down, and very angry. Everybody I looked at made me sick. At least when I was younger waiting all those years for my dad, I had hope to finally have him come and be in my life. Now it felt like I had just got cracked in the head with the reality knowing, that I would never see him again for the rest of my life. In just three weeks' time, my dad had died, I found out **EVERYONE** around me was doing drugs, and lying to me about it, and my husband was gone, (after stealing all of my dad's stuff), and lying constantly. I lost my oldest son, and had two small children that I really was not mentally able to care for. I was completely fucked up in the head. I moved out and took the kids, even though it was my house I just knew Donnie would not leave, and I did not want to be around him.

Then one night angry, crazy, and drinking, I decided the best revenge would be for me to get high too. I never did anything but stay home, cook, and clean, and take care of my kid, and husband, while everyone else was doing whatever. I thought this would show them, they will see how I feel. I went and did heroin. Well, guess what? When your whole family are addicts, and you are fucked up in the head anyway, you stand a pretty good chance of becoming an addict pretty quick: and I did. I think I became addicted the first time I tried it. I got a little bit scared because I knew I was liking it too much, and doing it too often so I decided to move out of town. I moved to Clinton, Illinois. I had called my sister Renee, and told her I was doing drugs, she came and picked me up, bless her heart, as I needed help so bad. Renee is two years younger than me, Penny, Annie, my stepmom already lived in Clinton. It was kind of cool there, and I felt a change of atmosphere might just be what I needed.

So of course, Donnie showed up after I had been there about a month. Everything pretty well sucked. I was staying with Renee, her husband, and 3 kids while I found an apartment. I did not know anyone, at first, but Renee and Annie took me out bar hopping and having fun. Renee is so kindhearted and it seemed like we fell in love with each other's kids instantly. We had lived far away from each other all those years, and did not even know each other. We went through a lot of stuff together later, and got close. I hate to think what would have happened to me if I had stayed in Kansas City. I doubt that I would be here today, that is for sure. I did not get to see Bug as much as I wanted to, and even though I knew I was a basket case, I wanted him back **SO** bad. All I did was drink, go to the bars and try to kill myself. I tore up every picture I had of my dad, cut my arms up so bad I think I got over a hundred stitches. I hated myself, and Donnie got to where he could not even sleep at night because he had to watch me all the time. I don't even know how many times I was in the hospital for cutting on myself. I just could not stand all the pain inside of me. I was not even really trying to kill myself most of the time. Basically I just hated myself, and hurt too bad to function. I was for real," crazy", I did not know what I was doing half the time. I am pretty sure no one expected me to survive this hell that was my world. However, I did make it through obviously.

I loved my kids very much, and I don't know how to even explain it. They were little, and had to see all this, and of course didn't understand what was wrong with their mother. Because of me, their childhood was starting to be as bad as mine was. I hated myself and just could not function. Donnie started back to the bars, and hitting me again. I had so many black eyes, so often, my daughter who was in kindergarten by this point, called me a raccoon. That was her nickname for me, she did not know any better, and that is pretty sad. I had to walk her back and forth to school, wait out in front with the other parents, and always with one eye or the other black. It was so humiliating, and as usual no one talked to me of course. What does one say to someone like that? By this point I was tired of sitting at home waiting for him to get done doing, whatever he was doing, so I was out every chance I got too. I was going to get my ass beat anyway, and I was sick of it. I pulled a lot of his own shit, on his ass by this point. Renee and I could not be trusted to go check the mail together or we'd be gone for 2 days. We got in a lot of trouble, got arrested together on Christmas Eve once. We had a lot of fun though. It was about time after all those years having to sit at home and wait on somebody, that I was the one out, and he was the one setting home waiting. He didn't much care for it any more than I had. Donnie started getting arrested shortly after we got there, and still never paid any bills. We just moved somewhere, and stayed until they evicted us, and then moved again.

He disappeared most of the time, and slept with members of my family. I started going to college. Donnie was so mad and did not want me to go. I guess he was afraid if I bettered myself I might leave him. I stayed beat up, and missed classes because of it, or he just wouldn't come home on the nights I was supposed to go to school. I had all the kids so of course I couldn't go. I passed some really hard classes that most of the people dropped out of just because, I was very determined and wouldn't let him win that battle. I have not graduated from college yet, but it is a goal that is very important to me. We ended up staying there in Clinton for a couple years. Donnie had a lot of warrants for old domestic battery charges, DUI's and bad checks. It was a small town and everyone knew him, so we moved back by St. Louis. Well, I moved back by St. Louis, and he went to prison for 10 months. While he was gone I stayed with my sister Heather.

Her husband Lee, was killed while driving, and high on Heroin in a car accident. Shortly after, I moved back to St. Louis. Heather was living by herself and not doing so hot. My sister was my best friend, and I loved her kids like my own. I also got to doing drugs really bad there. First, my sister sold meth, and I got a little bit caught up in that, until I found out what was in it. I really didn't care for it much. I also had a cousin who earned around a $1,000 a day stealing stuff, he didn't like getting high alone, so we were hanging around all the time. I ended up with a 2 gram of heroin habit per day, and was a mess. He brought it all home, and I rarely even left the house. I probably weighed 90 lbs. and looked horrible.

Donnie got out of prison, and came right back over to where I was living, and now we just got high together. It was an interesting life. Donnie, and Billy Jr. went out to make money all day, while I stayed home and took care of the kids, and the house. My cousin went to prison shortly after, because he was apparently robbing all the stores blind. We had two small children living in a cheap motel, or wherever someone might let us sleep for the night. We were for real, bums. We moved all over the place from one piece of shit apartment to the next. Sometimes we had no water, stove or fridge, hot as hell, or cold as ice, just anyplace we were not sleeping outside. We moved so much the kids missed seven months of school, because you have to have current utilities and proof of address to enroll. We never stayed anywhere long enough to have those things. History was repeating itself here. I ended up taking Amanda, and Donnie Jr. back to Clinton. Donnie however, stayed down in St. Louis. I did not want to live like that anymore.

It was a hard new start with two little kids, and trying to recover from a heroin habit. I was going through serious heroin withdrawals when I first got there for about 2 weeks. I could not function very well at all. All I did to help the situation was move but, geography doesn't fix an addiction problem. I met a nice guy named Jim, he took really good care of the kids, and just treated them like his own. We were starting to be a family, and things were going pretty good. The kids had their own rooms, it was peaceful, they were very happy, and I got to see Bug regularly. Of course, that made me very happy, because I missed him so much. My stepmom Annie lived close by, and was happy to hook me up with a drug dealer. Then my sister Heather moved up with me, and then one of my cousins. I started doing drugs again, drinking all the time. I don't know if I would have done better on my own, but I was not ready to have all the people I had been getting high with in St Louis to come and move in with me. I was still crazy and suicidal because of my dad, so I was like a psycho tornado, in and out of hospitals, jail and rehab. All this time I was running around doing these things and I don't even really remember. My kids were there for so much of it I wish they didn't remember either, but it just don't work like that. I did not consciously say I don't care what they are going through, and I did love them with all my heart. My head was just a mess. I overdosed a couple times on heroin to where I was legally dead, and was taken away from the house in an ambulances, and police cars. All the while I'm sure they were crying, scared, and angry as hell.

I was giving them the same childhood as I had. That is the biggest regret I have deep down in my soul, because I love them so much I'd die for them. They deserved so much more than what they got. I can never undo the pain and, anguish I caused. All I can do is tell them I love them with all my heart, and I am so sorry. It was never that I didn't care about them enough, I just couldn't control my crazy mind. The alcohol and drugs numbed the pain so I didn't feel like that all the time. If I could have one wish in my entire life it would be that they don't follow in the path as their parents. Poor Jim, he was a really nice guy, although he had a little temper and flaws like any other man in the world but he sure did not deserve all the crap I put him through.

In 2001, I got arrested with my sister Heather for possession of drug paraphernalia, and I ended up getting 2 years in prison for that. I had to serve 5 months of that sentence, and a felony drug conviction. Now, I was in no way innocent that day we got arrested, but none of those drugs in that car, on that day were mine. I was arrested because I was the driver, and after I missed one court appearance, I had a $2,500 cash bond I could not pay. The judge said he would drop the warrant if I would plead guilty and receive probation, which I did. However, I violated that probation which is why I ended up in prison. So I may have not been guilty in that particular circumstance, but I had done enough other ignorant shit even I wouldn't try to complain about it. I had moved down closer to St. Louis because I had warrants and I did not know what to do with my family while I was away. I could not find a place to live so we were staying in a hotel in Troy Illinois I guess I was just plotting my next move. I did not have anyone to turn to or help me. Then one day I was sitting in the hotel room waiting for Amanda, and Donnie Jr. to get off the bus from school. Bugs dad was about to drop him off for a weekend visit. Amanda's grandma was coming to pick her up for their first weekend visit. My son Donnie Jr. came in first, then the police came in to arrest me. Amanda got dropped off next from the school bus, her first weekend visit with her grandparents and the dad she never met, that lasted 6 months. Bugs dad showed up next to drop him off, and walked into all of this, and said he would stay with Donnie Jr. and Amanda until they got picked up.

Then he took Bug back home. I know they went through hell while I was gone, but it worked out ok for Amanda. She got to be close to her dad, and she was alright. Bug and Donnie Jr. had a very bad time while I was gone. I did not see Bug the whole time I was away, I know how bad it hurt him that I was gone and I think he might have had less love for me that year, and I don't blame him.

Donnie Jr. was so little, he stayed at first with the creep I was seeing when I got arrested, and went through a really rough time I did not have anywhere else for him to go. I know I am a total loser for putting him through what I did, you don't have to tell me. Then Jim ended up getting Donnie Jr. for the last couple months, and he was ok, but really sad. I got to see him, Jim brought him up to the prison for visits, and he was so little he would just lay on my lap throughout the entire visit. The whole time was a freakin nightmare. I got out, got the kids back around. Things were ok I got an apartment for the four of us, and it was really good for a while. Then I started hanging around people again who did all the stuff I was not supposed to do. I still did drugs and drank like crazy, somehow I completed my parole. Donnie and I got back together every now and then, but he would hit me again and go back to prison again, I divorced him in 2003, after he hit me one more time and the police just came and took him to jail, I was really tired of all of his shit by then. I started seeing someone else. The kids and I ended up moving out there with him for quite some time. He lived on a farm and the kids had a lot of room to run around, they had a good time we were all pretty happy at first. When Bug was 15 I figured out that our custody papers were not even legal, and I had had custody of him the whole time. He had driven his stepmom so crazy, they needed to not be around each other for a while. So I got my baby boy back, I was so freakin happy. Things were ok, I guess, I was living in the country with all my kids. We had some good times. I think they really enjoyed it.

My sister Heather had been staying up here in Clinton, IL for a couple of years and she was doing so much better than she had been doing in St Louis. She had stopped taking all those pills like she was, and seemed to be living a normal, happy life. She still had not got custody of her kids back from my mom yet.

She was doing well, and had begun trying to reopen the case my mom had filed to get her children back. She had received papers from Social Security wanting her to do something to renew her file. She was unable to do all they asked, because of her depression issues so they stopped sending her a Social Security check, which in turn stopped her health insurance. She had gotten a prescription for Prozac, an antidepressant, and was taking it, but when they stopped her insurance she was forced to stop taking the medication abruptly. When that happens it causes severe emotional problems.

I was at home one day, on June 27, 2003, when the phone rang. It was Heather's boyfriend's sister, saying I needed to come over I got there and I had barely stepped out of my car, my door was still open and Heathers boyfriend was waiting on the sidewalk. He told me "your sisters fucking dead", that is how I was told that my best friend, hero, parents, sister, everything in my world was gone forever. She had hung herself on the doorway and had not even been removed yet. Well I was **NOT** ok as one might understand. Heather had no life insurance and I had no idea how I was going to pay for a funeral. My mom did not seem to care. The funeral home actually told me that I had until four o'clock that evening to make the arrangements. I was so mad I just said, "Or what, are you going to throw her out?" I was so upset I could not function at all. I stayed in bed for a month while my kids survived on frozen pizza, and cereal. I did the best I could during that time. My mom finally decided to help me with my sister's burial.

I'm not sure which one was most traumatizing for me, losing my dad, or my sister. I was a freakin mental train wreck.

I was still messed up over losing my sister, and six months later it was Christmas time in 2003. I had a few people over to celebrate. Bug, and Donnie Jr. went to visit their dad, and somehow Amanda did not want to go. Maybe, because our next door neighbor had a 17 or 18 yr. old son. They had went to visit relatives and left him home alone. Our families were pretty good friends. I was a single mom and so was she, we leaned on each other, helped each other out, and just talked. I invited her son over to hang out with Amanda and have dinner with us. The kids' bedrooms were upstairs, all the grown-ups were downstairs hanging out. I went up at one point in the evening to go to the bathroom and check on the kids. Amanda was still 12 years old, I really did not think there was anything going on with her, and this guy. I guess I was just stupid, he was like part of our family and I trusted him. When I went in her room I could see that there was something going on, and threw him out of our house. The next few weeks were a mess. It turned out she really had been talking to him and thought she was in love with him. He kept trying to come around, she would try to sneak around. Then on January 14, 2004, it was Amanda's 13th birthday. I was having just a little family party, with me and the kids. The 17 yr. old boy had been calling the house still. I got her a bunch of clothes for her birthday, and some other stuff. She was going upstairs in her room to try stuff on, and then she would come back so I could make sure the jeans were not too tight or whatever. I went up to talk to her once about something and we got to arguing about her boyfriend. I told her he was just too old for her. I was not going to change my mind, she would never be allowed to be with him. I was sitting on her bed and she was lying across my lap, and I rubbed her hair and told her I loved her, but it was never going to be with this boy. She said she loved me too, and we bickered a little more, we did that quite frequently so that was no big deal. I left her to cool off a bit. We were supposed to rent a movie and we picked

"Bruce Almighty". I had her cake and a dinner I cooked for us. I had just started the movie. Bug was 15, Donnie Jr. was 9 I think. I gave her about 20 minutes and decided to go check on he again, because she was being so quiet. When I walked up into her room, I did not see or hear anything, I looked in the bathroom, and Donnie Jr. 's room, I was thinking, where could she have gone? There was no way out from up there, and I was sitting by the door downstairs, thinking she couldn't have gotten past me. I am not sure why, but then I opened her closet door to look and see if she was hiding, or what was going on, I found my daughter hanging by a dog leash tied up to the bar on the closet.

Reality, was so far gone from me, and in slow motion, and shock I tried to untie it, but it was too tight. I picked her limp body up to relieve the pressure from her neck, and yelled for Bug to bring me a knife so I could cut it. I am not sure if Bug or Donnie Jr. called 911 while I was holding Amanda up, but Bug had to cut her down. I have always felt horrible that I made him do that, but I could not hold her up and cut it, and I was too scared to let go of her. Bug tried to perform CPR on her, while we waited for the ambulance. All I remember doing was screaming at Donnie Jr. to go in the other room because I did not want him to see her. I am still thinking she is going to be ok. I thought she was just mad, and trying to scare me since my sister had just committed suicide 6 months before. Police, and paramedics showed up and made us stay in the house and did not want us to talk to anyone. I didn't know what was going on so I kept asking why they were not taking her to the hospital. Detectives came and talked to me, one took me in the kitchen and asked me some questions, I told them about the guy she had been seeing, then they told me I had to go with him to the hospital to give consent for treatment. The police took my kids down to the police station to ask some more questions. They really did not want us there when they had to wheel her past us out of the house. When I walked in the hospital, I saw my sister Renee waiting out in the hall. I kind of in a daze, as they led me down a hall and into an empty room. I was still thinking Amanda and she was going to be fine. I wanted to go in, and yell at her for scaring me so bad.

The chaplain and a doctor sat me down and informed me that they had not been able to save my daughter, she didn't make it. I have never in my life heard someone scream such a loud heart wrenching, horrified, scream and It was coming from me. It felt like someone had just violently ripped a cheese grater across my soul. I would never have, even imagined a human being could hurt so badly, and I, would not ever wish a pain like that on my worst enemy. I said, no that is not true, I just came to sign some papers. Then, two of my sisters, my sons, and my ex-husband came in the room, and I had to tell my sons that they had lost their sister. They both looked so sad, lost, hurt, and helpless. The horror, and emptiness, and loss so evident in their young eyes it almost changed their color. They have never looked the same again. The pain reached all the way down into their being, down into their very souls and hearts. We stood together the three of us, and just hugged, there wasn't really much to say. I had to go plan another funeral. Amanda had a huge funeral with more people than I had ever seen at a funeral, her school had excused all the students that day to attend, her story was on the evening news about how a young girl committed suicide on her 13th birthday over a grown man who wanted to date her. I really tried to keep us together the best I could, but I was **NOT** ok. I tried to keep our little family as functional as possible, but I was a complete nutcase by this point. I remember when we left the hospital, Bugs dad had left work immediately and drove up to be with us at the hospital. No one wanted to go back to the house were Amanda had just died, so we went back to my ex-boyfriends house to stay. When we first pulled up we all got out of the car, and Bug just stayed in the backseat, and said, "She was my best friend I don't know what to do". He was a total mess after that, he did not know if he was coming or going. Donnie Jr. was so small and sad. I don't think he ever smiled the same again after that. He had a look in his eyes like part of him had died too. Like all the spirit had been sucked right out of both of them. I don't know what I looked like, but I know I drank too much, and all I did was stumble around from day to day. I didn't know what I was doing.

People still think my behavior was strange I guess. I have heard some of them making fun of how I acted, but I didn't know what I was doing, all I knew was I could not stand to feel what my heart was going through. I would do anything to not feel, as usual I am not perfect, and made a lot of mistakes, but unless you have been in them same shoes I was walking around in at that time, you just go ahead and keep your judgments to yourself. No one has any idea how you would be, or what you would do in any of these situations.

I got arrested for various assault charges because I was angry as hell anyway. Donnie Jr. was 9 yrs. old, and had just watched his sister die in front of him when and he came from school, and told me that some older kids were talking shit about his sister. They were saying his sister was a ho, and about all they had done to her the night before. They did not know Amanda was his sister. I went down there and told them not to talk shit to my son about his sister because she had just died. They told me they knew Amanda and did not mean to say anything bad. **WE** were all good until their dad came outside and pushed me, and I beat the crap out of him, I got arrested for aggravated battery, and mob action. When I got to the jail I had on an ankle bracelet that was red white and blue, the color of my kid's birthstones. The officer made me take it off to get booked in. I was mad still and threw it over the counter, and it bounced off the counter and hit the cop in his face. It was like a 1/4 ounce piece of plastic and did not even leave a mark. So they also charged me with aggravated battery on a police officer. Even though he testified at my trial that he was not injured and it did not hurt. I asked him later why he did that, and he said he didn't think they would do anything to me about it.

While I was in jail I lost custody of both of my sons. DCFS had come to the jail, and said they did not believe I was able to take care of them at this point, and needed a **LOT** of therapy. Bug went to his dads', Donnie Jr. went to his aunts. I was only in there 8 days, and walked out homeless, all of my kids gone, knowing my sons hearts were broken. I did decide at this point in my life that I just had to stop trying to hurt myself. They had been through too much and did not need to worry about losing their mom anymore. I did not cut myself again, and stopped doing heroin. I did not want them to worry they were going to lose me too. I went to a doctor to try to get some help in quitting heroin. He gave me a drug called Suboxone. It makes you not feel dope sick, as you go through the withdrawal process. It also does something else, if you do use heroin while you are on Suboxone it throws you into very painful and violent withdrawals, (I had to learn that the hard way of course) The state's attorney had arrested Amanda's boyfriend and charged him with criminal sexual predatory assault and since there was more than a 5 yr. age difference, that made it a felony. He stayed in jail for 6 months, the state wanted to nail his ass to the wall. I was expected to testify on Amanda's behalf, and I was in a mental hospital the week the trial was scheduled so they had to let him go. I just couldn't even talk about her still and trying to relive the whole story at that time was more than I was able to bear. That was the last time I was in the hospital for hurting myself. I had to go to rehab, counseling, domestic violence classes, and another group called Survivors of Suicide. It took me a year, but I got my children back. We were together again. Of course I was very happy, it was so hard on all three of us to be apart. Donnie Jr. was still so little. I was doing much better, but still nuts. There did not seem to be a therapy that could fix the way I felt. I did get Amanda a headstone for her next Christmas present. It is a rose colored heart shaped and on the front it says, "beautiful angel we love and miss you so much love Mom, Bug and Donnie Jr.,". A precious moments angel is pouring small hearts down the front of it. AMANDA GRACE NOVAK Jan 14th, 1991—Jan 14th 2004. and at the very bottom.. anmmbff (for Amanda's best friend it is their initials).

I hated celebrating birthdays, I'm not sure after Amandas I was scared. I would not really discipline them. I felt I had tried to discipline my daughter and I lost her I was just too scared to do anything. I did end up going back to prison for about 10 months on the assault charges I had. Bug was 19 at this time, and Donnie Jr. was 15 he stayed with my sister Renee, and a friend of mine. It was while I was in prison this time, I tried to call my sister Renee, and she, and Rose had to tell me that my stepmom, Annie, had committed suicide the same way Heather and Amanda had. Of course that was horrible and even worse for me because I was locked away from everyone. I did use the time I was in there to better myself. I also received 45 days off of my sentence, but I got a lot out of it too, and worked very hard to try to get myself together. First I signed up for the drug treatment program in order to have my sentence reduced. And I had a drug counselor, psychiatrist, and a couple of other therapists at my beck and call so I decided to use every waking moment in there learning to heal from my emotional wounds process all of the pain I had endured, and make myself stronger when I got out. If I was awake I was working on myself. I learned a lot, and I healed a lot. It did change some things about me.

When I got out I moved Donnie Jr., and myself back to St. Louis. Bug had met someone by this point, and was planning his wedding, and the birth of his son. So Donnie Jr., and I got an apartment, and tried to do ok, and we were. I still drank too much beer, but I did not go out, or use drugs, and I did not go crazy, and try to hurt myself anymore. That was about the best I could offer as far as normal went. Donnie Jr. however, kept getting in trouble, and went to see his dad for Thanksgiving that year. Donnie and I got to talking again, and I told him," hey, your son is driving me nuts, you need to come and take care of your kid". We had not even seen Donnie in five years since he had been in prison, or just off somewhere. Donnie said ok. I knew he was coming but I did not tell Donnie Jr., just for fun. I was sitting out on our couch watching television, and Donnie Jr. came out of his room and said, "hey did you know my dad's outside", he said. I was laughing, and I said, "Well yeah, go let him in".

That day, Donnie moved back in, and took the weight of the world off of my shoulders. Donnie Jr. had to have counseling, family counseling, parents of bad kids groups, court worker, and court dates. All kinds of different stuff, and I was having such a hard time doing it by myself. I didn't drive, and I am terrible with directions, so it was hard for me to take a bus to all these places. I am not complaining at all, I would do anything for my son, it was just hard for me. Donnie took over all of it, and I was so relieved. He stayed and decorated the house for Christmas, and went to church with us Christmas morning, opened presents, and we had a big family holiday meal. It was awesome, and Donnie Jr. was so happy. He finally got his dad back. Then Donnie Jr. got put on house arrest, and violated it. He had to go back to jail. Donnie at least went with me for visits. The court dates, however, and anything that was too hard for me he took care of. We were getting along ok. Laughing, hanging out, and finding a way to survive, and exist. I had loved that man SOOO much and he had put me through hell. He really had changed in his old age I guess. He did not hit me, he listened to me about everything I was upset about, apologized, and even admitted to his family that he really had beat the crap out of me all those years As one remembers, back then, he told everyone I was just crazy and he was not doing anything. We really got along good, better than we ever had. It was like I was finally good friends with the love of my life.

Bug had been married by this point, and gave us our first grandson, Isaac. I still hadn't done drugs since that day back in 2004. Donnie said he had been clean for a long time also, but we would talk about it every now, and then which is really all it takes when one is an addict. Even though he claimed he had been clean he still had our old dope dealers' phone number in his wallet. Then one day he called him, and went to go buy us some Heroin. We were just going to do a little bit and hang out.

We actually did it a couple times, but we were not use to it like we had been back in the day. We had gotten remarried by this point. Donnie Jr. was still in jail. It was on June 25th, 2010, when Donnie came home with $50 worth of heroin for us to split. He did his part of the drug, while I was messing around. It was about 10 minutes or so after him, when I walked out of the bathroom, and found Donnie leaning on our dining room table, and looked like he was having a seizure. I grabbed him and leaned him back on the table so he would not hit his head, but he was not moving. I had seen a lot of people do this before when they were doing Heroin, and Donnie would just put cold water on their face, and they were ok. I tried that, but it didn't work, I really did not want to call 911, because he was on parole, and I did not want him to get in trouble. I could not, wake him up so I called, the police to come and help me. The dispatcher told me to pick him up off of the dining room table, and put him on the floor, and I did. Then they told me to keep performing CPR until the paramedics arrived, which I did, by the time police, and paramedics got there, I was starting to lose consciousness myself. They called a second ambulance for me also. On the way to the hospital I was given Narcan, a drug that counteracts the effects of the Heroin. I went from unconscious to wide awake instantly, with the sudden knowledge that my husband had died. I could just feel that he was gone. They kept using codes on the paramedic's radios, and were trying to keep from telling me at the time because they were trying to get my heart rate back to normal, it was supposed to be 70, and mine was 150. I got to the hospital, and was hooked up to some machines, and hoses, I guess still confused and hazy. They sent a chaplain in before a doctor. He asked me how I was doing, and I was just staring at the wall not saying anything. I told him I knew my husband had just died, but that I didn't want anyone to tell me.

I just didn't want it to be real, I wanted it to not be true. Doctors came in, and told me they needed a family member to call, still not telling me about Donnie. I knew he was there in the hospital too, but no one said anything about him and I couldn't ask. I could not bring myself to say it out loud. I felt it, I knew. When they asked who they could call I was telling them I did not want anyone. Finally I gave them the phone number for one of my neighbors who could go to my apartment and get Bugs phone number. He was the only person I wanted to see. Donnie Jr. was still in a juvenile correctional facility, I knew I could not call him. My neighbor broke in my apartment, and got my cell phone, and called my relatives, Donnie's mother, and the whole family. She then came up to see me in the hospital. She even drove to the jail Donnie Jr. was in, and told him that his dad had died, and that his mom was in cardiac distress. I don't know if I ever thanked her for all of that, I didn't know how to do anything right then. I don't know how I would have called anyone. I was barefoot, wearing some snoopy pajama pants, and one of Donnie's shirts that was soaking wet from holding, and moving him trying to save him after I had tried to pour water on him. I obviously did not have my cell phone which had all of our family's phone numbers stored in it.

It seemed like all at once my room was full of people Bug, and his wife, the jail people had even brought Donnie Jr. there. He walked in the room and just laid across me and cried louder, and longer than I had ever seen him do. The doctor came in too, break it to me that my husband had not made it. I did not say a word. I had felt it down inside me as soon as I woke up. They let me go where he was to say good bye to him. I could not even stand up. My husband was really gone. It was really hard on both boys, harder on Donnie Jr. of course, because it was the only dad he had. He had waited his whole life to have his dad just to lose him shortly after to a Heroin overdose. We had both lost our sisters to suicide, and both had crazy mothers. It is eerie the similarities between the two of us. One huge difference is how very much his mother loves him, and I fully admit I was so wrong, and apologize from the bottom of my heart. I will always be there to support and love my boys. I need them more than anything in the whole world. I had to stay in the hospital for maybe seven or eight days. Donnie's family was trying to make the funeral arrangements but could not set the date of the services until I got released from the hospital. Donnie Jr. and Bug came up, and stayed with me every day, somebody from the jail came up there with Donnie Jr. all day every day and let him be with me. I was very scared, and very sad. When they were not there I just stared at the wall in silence.

Finally I told the doctor if he didn't release me so I could bury my husband I was just going to walk out. They released me that day, I had to wait downstairs for my husband's personal effects of a $187 and a metro link receipt. Then, I went back home, alone to sit in the room he had died in. It still did not seem real. When we had his funeral, Donnie Jr. also was brought to the service and both of my sons were pall bearers. I don't think I have ever been so proud of them. I cannot even imagine how hard it must have been for them to carry him to his final resting place, but they never even flinched. The just walked through the whole ordeal and loved their father until the end like men. I did part of the eulogy because I did not want everyone to only remember Donnie Novak as some mean guy who fought in the bars, beat his wife, went to prison and died of a Heroin overdose. In that year he had come back home he became the best father he could, and a very proud grandfather. I have never in my life seen that man smile the way he did when he held, and looked at Isaac. It was like all the mean just melted off of his face, and it was love at first sight. He was a pa-pa, and he even tutored the neighbor kids in math, because of his construction work experience, and was very good at it. He was quick to play with all the kids, helped the neighbor ladies fix things, and everyone called him uncle Donnie. He was a man to be proud of.

By this time he was unable to find work in construction where the real money was. My husband got a job making minimum wage at, Jack in the Box. I was more proud of him for earning that little minimum wage paycheck than I had ever been when he earned a construction worker wage. I knew he hated it, and thought it was demeaning, but he did it anyway for us. I am very proud of the man he did become. I forgave every hurt we ever had. I will never forget the love we had. It is still really hard for me to talk about him very much, he took another little piece of my heart with him when he left too.

It has been four years now, and Donnie Jr. has a son named Jacob Thomas, We both live back in Clinton Il., but Bug got divorced, and lives down in southern Illinois. We still all have each other, love each other, and are close. I don't think we will ever forget the way we have felt over the years, and how we needed each other so much. After all it seemed like, we were all we have. My sister Renee finally married a nice man named Jonathan, and her sons are grown with many grandchildren for her. They seem to be happy and I hope he takes good care of my sister because she deserves it. She is an amazing woman who has been there for me so often in my life, I just don't know what I would have done without her. I love her with all my heart and am very thankful to her. She has **ALWAYS** been an awesome aunt, sister, and friend to me. Rose also married a wonderful man named Chester, he is the closest thing I have to Lee, Heathers husband, who was such a good brother to me. He loves me like a real sister, not just like he has to, and they have two boys I love so very much, some cartoon characters, they are.

Penny also married Jeremiah, and they have two critters of their own also a beautiful teenage girl, and a rambunctious boy. They live in the country raising chickens, and growing some of their own food It is a quiet, pleasant life, and I think she is pretty happy. I love my sisters so, and treasure every moment, memory, laugh, and hug I was blessed with. I spent all of the last year recovering from a bad car wreck, and ended up with Congestive Heart Failure, and a Pulmonary Embolism. I had a lot of good friends pray for me, and I am in therapy now to regain some physical strength, and lessen the pain hopefully. My sisters and Chester took care of me very well while I was in the hospital, the girls came up and gave me a bath, visited, brought me all kinds of wonderful treats. It made me feel loved. Chester came up to spend time with me every day, and snuck all kinds of stuff in for me that I was not allowed to have. It did not look like I was going to make it for a while. The hospital had sent the chaplain up to see me and was getting ready to put me on life support.

I started to miraculously getting better so, **APPARENTLY**, God does not want me yet. I still must have stuff to do down here, which is ok with me. The kids too, had to stay, and take care of me when I got home from the hospital, and it was very hard. Some days, I just think to myself. I don't believe I know one other person who has survived all this much hardship in life. You would expect me to be that person locked away forever in some asylum setting over in the corner sucking on a crayon or something. However, I am really positive, upbeat, and happy. I created an internet group called Addiction Survival. It is to help educate people on the dangers of Heroin abuse, and inform them the signs to look for in their loved ones if they suspect they might be using, we share what we have been through, explain how we made it, and give support to each other. It is 2014 when I complete this book and, I have begun a new relationship with Jim again. We are very happy so far. Life is good and I think we can be happy, and take pretty good care of each other in our old age.

I have high hopes for the boys, and my futures. I do have two main goals in life that means a lot to me to complete. One of them is writing this book, that I called, "Nobody's Daughter", because for the most of my life that is what I was. I never had anyone who was happy to be my parent, and I have lost more people that I love than any one person should ever have too. I will always get back up, and keep moving forward as long as my little heart keeps beating. After all the medical tests I have had this last few months they show I no longer have, Congestive Heart Failure, and the blood clot in my lung has dissolved. I can only thank God for this because no one else can explain it. I am very thankful to God for everything He does for me, and has done. So why did I write this book and bare my soul, and show every flaw, mistake, and weakness I have? I know sometime, somewhere, there is going to be someone, who is going through some really hard things in their life. They may think they can't make it through, and life is just too hard. I just want them to know, that one really does have the strength down deep inside them to make it. One just has to dig deep, and find a positive in every situation, and focus on that to survive. Even with all the people I have lost in my life, I am so thankful for having the opportunity to know them, and create the memories we will always cherish.

For all of the mistakes, and bad decisions I made, I can only hope my boys will learn how to deal with life better than I did. Please learn from my mistakes sons, and not repeat them. Just slow down, take care of yourselves, and those around you. Whenever you think God has left you to deal with all of your trauma on your own, know that He has not left you, and that He is not the one responsible for choices and mistakes people make. God is who helps you be able to make it through the pain. I apologize from the bottom of my heart for the mistakes I have made, and any hurt I have caused, especially to my sons. I truly hope they can forgive me, and love me anyway. However, it is time for me to lift my head up, and quit living in the past, and feeling guilty for things I cannot ever change. I can never make the hurt go away, but I do love you with every beat of my heart, and I am sincerely sorry. You deserved so much better. For anyone, anywhere who is going through a load of unfairness, in your life, believe me when I say you are able to get through this even if it does not seem possible right now. Maybe it was stubbornness, pride, but mostly it was strength, and determination to show my sons they can be strong enough to find a way through anything. I also had to be strong enough to survive because they could not have handle losing me. For a long time I did not even want to be here, life just hurt too much. I kept going for my children, and they are the reason I live, and breathe, because I love them with all my heart.

I hope they know this, and find a way to forgive all the many mistakes I made with them. I definitely do not want to repeat my mistakes with their own children.

Finally, my second goal is to finish college, as I would like to be certified as a drug counselor. I plan to start working on that now that I have finished this book. I did not ever think I would ever get this far, but I did. With the grace, mercy, and love of God I have survived what was my life. So if you think you cannot go anymore, or take anymore please don't ever give up. You never know what is up the road waiting for you. Peace to all.

Printed in the United States
By Bookmasters